Egon Ronay was born in Hungary and educated in Budapest. He emigrated to England in 1946 and opened his own restaurant, The Marquee in Knightsbridge, in 1952, which was described by the *Daily Telegraph* as 'London's most food-perfect small restaurant'.

He founded Egon Ronay's Guides in 1957, wrote a weekly column in the *Daily Telegraph* and *Sunday Telegraph* from 1954–1960, and the *London Evening News* from 1968–1974. He now has a regular column in *The Sunday Times*.

Egon Ronay was the first non-French member of l'Académie des Gastronomes. He was awarded the Médaille de la Ville de Paris by Jacques Chirac in 1983 and was made a Chevalier de l'Ordre du Mérite Agricole in 1987.

He lives with his wife Barbara in Berkshire and in London.

Egon Ronay

The unforgettable dishes of my life

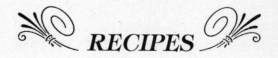 *RECIPES*

SPHERE BOOKS LTD

A SPHERE Book

First published in Great Britain by
Egon Ronay Publications (Cookery) Limited 1989
Published by Sphere Books Ltd 1991
Copyright © Egon Ronay 1989

The right of Egon Ronay to be identified as author of this work
has been asserted by him in accordance with
the Copyright, Designs and Patents Act 1988.

Typeset by Leaper & Gard Ltd, Bristol
Printed and bound in Great Britain by
The Guernsey Press Co. Ltd, Guernsey, Channel Islands.

ISBN 0747409374

A Division of
Macdonald & Co (Publishers) Ltd
Orbit House
1 New Fetter Lane
London EC4A 1AR
A member of Maxwell Macmillan Pergamon Publishing Corporation

To the memory of my Mother and Father,
two of the greatest restaurateurs I have known

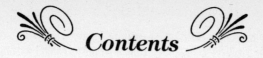

Contents

FAN-ASSISTED OVENS

All dishes can, of course, be prepared in a fan-assisted oven but the
temperatures in this book might have to be converted and reduced to those
recommended by the oven manufacturers in their conversion tables. Very
little pre-heating time may be needed, except possibly for yeast-based or
soufflé dishes.

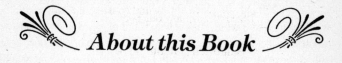

About this Book

During 28 years of publishing my hotel and restaurant guides, I have resisted many approaches to write and publish cookery books, on the ground that my organisation was pre-occupied with four annual guides, and cookery books would have deflected our attention considerably. A more personal reason was the motivation behind the proposals. It was suggested, rightly or wrongly, that my name would sell cookery books and that their contents and the contribution these could make to gastronomy in this country were beside the point. Since I have never written or published anything purely for financial gain, I declined.

Now that my guidebooks have another publisher, I have embarked upon publishing cookery books with the firm proviso that they will be unorthodox as far as their subject matter, approach and design are concerned. Rather than trying to persuade publishers, whose blinkers are often their balance sheets, that they need not stick to well-trodden paths, I set up, together with a colleague from my guidebook days, a company to publish cookery books. They will conform to our ideal of quality first, which, we believe, also happens to be the safest way to viability.

Given my family background, this attitude of mine is quite natural. It took root when my grandfather built a 120-room hotel in Pöstyén, Northern Hungary, in 1910, and was continued by my father, who owned and ran five of the best restaurants in Budapest between the two wars. I carried on in the same vein as a restaurateur for 25 years and eventually as publisher of my guidebooks. Round the family table, and later when my father started to take me to his meetings just to listen, there was not a single instance I can recall when profitability was discussed. The subjects were invariably the improvement of food, service and amenities, never the gain this would bring. It was always assumed that the pursuit of excellence, and being better than the competition, would automatically bring the financial results. It most certainly did in my father's case: he became the fifth-biggest taxpayer in Budapest.

Two other branches of my family were also in the restaurant profession, so it is hardly surprising that I have always been preoccupied with the subject of food. Not only do I love eating and cooking, but, above all, I love talking about food and wine. That is why I find most cookery books somewhat abstract. Recipes on their own, without a sense of occasion, people, atmosphere or gastronomic background, are in a vacuum comparable to sex without love: while it certainly has its points, it is not the same. The single-minded concentration on the clinical, stereotyped, dry instructions of recipes, without a thought for their joyful purpose, is a barren exercise. That's why Elizabeth David's books in this country and M.F.K. Fisher's in America stand out so much.

The idea for this particular book sprang from a curious twist in the way my memory works. I tend to associate events, even from my distant past, with the food I ate at the time, or before or afterwards. Conversely, certain dishes that have proved unforgettable always evoke the circumstances or events connected with them. This decided the form of the book. I wanted to recall the unforgettable dishes of my life and the memories associated with them. I have found the process a surprisingly emotional experience, sometimes quite unsettling, as it revived buried friends and relatives, long-forgotten flavours, places and restaurants that have radically changed or perhaps disappeared. This inclination to associate memories with food has made them all the more vivid and has strangely helped me to relive them with more realism.

The net cast itself wide. There is no common denominator in the sense that the recipes happen to represent cuisines of numerous countries and have, I hope, a diverse appeal. This coincides with my belief that the palate has no nationality: the view that only a specialist in, say, Indian or Creole cuisine can assess its quality is a fallacy. Good food is good food and there is nothing more to it. In this spirit, the catholic array of recipes, in any case dictated by my self-imposed terms of reference — the title of this book, reflects my lack of prejudice in any direction. And another thing: these dishes are for enjoyment, not to pander to present-day health terrorists. Many are from other culinary times, and it is perhaps just as well to take a rest from 'nouvelle' mousses and to stop casting cooks in the role of doctors.

The majority of the recipes are those we use at my home; many of them originate from my family's restaurants or have been collected over the years. A few are from chefs, not necessarily famous, in a number of countries, but tried out and adapted for home use. There were other dishes which, though certainly unforgettable, would have been too complicated to attempt except by very experienced cooks, so I have, reluctantly, left them out. I wanted the recipes to be practical and easily manageable, with a handful of exceptions — how could I have resisted, for example, publishing the intriguing process of stretching strudel pastry, even though few people would attempt it?

The role of my wife Barbara in this book has been enormously important. She has contributed many recipes of her own and helped in numerous other ways, including layouts, not to mention the reliability of her palate. I don't think I could have done it without her — a stock phrase, except in this case it's true. Equally significant were my colleagues, Nigel Jones, managing director of our new company, and Veronica Jones, another director with an admirable instinct for typography and layout. It is no small task for four people to write, edit, type, cook, actually set the text, design the book and arrange the illustrations, paper and printing — in other words to perform all the jobs that normally occupy a large staff.

Egon Ronay
May 1989

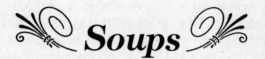

Soups

Barbara's Semi-clear Vegetable Soup

L ying in a hospital bed, after a successful operation and two days in intensive care, I was just beginning to get my appetite back. With nothing else pleasant to think about and utterly hating everything on the tray they kept bringing me (only the accompanying smile was palatable), I fantasized about wonderful consommés down the years: a clear, completely transparent essence made of beef at my last restaurant in Knightsbridge years ago; another, surfacing from the '60s, made of shell-fish in a now defunct restaurant — in Cornwall of all places.

I vividly remembered chicken consommé at my aunt's home on Sundays as a young boy, with flecks of telling little grease pools on top, through which improbably light, small, semolina dumplings kept bobbing up. Other ideas, unrealistic in the place I was, of light, creamy soups made of sorrel or watercress or chicken, added to my gastronomic — not to speak of my more serious — predicament.

To this poor patient it seemed incredible that the chef of one of London's most expensive private hospitals should be unable to produce anything edible. (When I finally whispered 'Very underdone omelette', it arrived sloshing about in a soup plate!! On top of it all, the unfortunate creature, knowing who I was, came up to see me, asking whether everything was satisfactory...)

And then I suddenly remembered something that my wife Barbara had concocted once, wanting to use up two pheasant carcasses, her imagination roping in the help of numerous herbs and bits of vegetable. I was saved: from then on she appeared daily, like an attractive and extremely smart version of a Mediterranean peasant woman, bearing the best things in life contained in a casserole over which the ends of several layers of colourful cloth were tied in a prettily arranged knot.

May you never need it as a similar relief.

BARBARA'S SEMI-CLEAR VEGETABLE SOUP

Serves 6

1 large carrot
1 large leek
1/2 turnip
1 small onion
1 pheasant, duck or chicken carcass
  (preferably 2 if you have them)
1 heaped tablespoon finely chopped
  parsley

1/2 level teaspoon dried thyme
1/2 level teaspoon dried sage
2 bayleaves
2 cloves garlic, crushed
6 juniper berries, crushed
1 pinch ground mace
2 chicken stock cubes
Salt and pepper to taste

Clean, peel and finely slice the carrot, leek, turnip and onion. If the vegetables are large, cut the slices into quarters. Place these in a large saucepan together with the carcass and remaining ingredients.

Dissolve the stock cubes in enough hot water to just cover the ingredients. Simmer on a hot stove for about 1 1/2 hours.

Remove the bayleaves and carcass and season to taste before serving.

The Black Bean Soup of New Orleans

Where races converge, interesting and unusual cuisines often develop. New Orleans is such a melting pot. A blend of Cajun cooking, basic American foods and a strong Creole influence has resulted in New Orleans cuisine with a character of its own.

It must have been much superior to what one finds there today. Promotional skills and tourist hype have watered down and corrupted original culinary values. The remnants are there and, I believe, professional commentators who could enthuse sincerely about New Orleans gastronomy 50 to 60 years ago. The legendary and huge Antoine's, for example, now packed with tourists, didn't have a queue, and their renowned speciality, Oysters Rothschild, was surely more sophisticated than its present-day incarnation. The city has become a disappointing venue for eating. Paul Prudhomme's Cajun cooking at K-Paul's still shines, but his 'blackened redfish' is now too widely vulgarised by others in America.

Nevertheless, Southern cooking is alive and well, even if it doesn't necessarily live in Louisiana restaurants. Take black bean soup. Not many people will disagree that one of the best versions can be found in New York at the Coach House, together with pecan pie and a gorgeously rich chocolate gâteau.

The Coach House is a good example of what draws me to a restaurant in New York. Excellent, French-orientated cooking is now easy to find — at a price — but you can get better in Europe. I prefer places with a feel of New York. They may not be the first preference of food bibles, but I head for Palm, the steak house with the unruly turmoil they call service; or another steak house, the wonderful Peter Luger, just across the Williamsburg Bridge, with unparalleled steaks and waiters perhaps a trifle too familiar (though I like them); and the Oyster Bar at Grand Central Station, a blend of Italy, France and Germany, which makes it really American.

THE BLACK BEAN SOUP OF NEW ORLEANS

Serves 8

10 oz (300 g) black beans
3 rashers smoked streaky bacon
1 medium onion
1 large stick celery
1 tablespoon oil
1½ level tablespoons flour
2 smoked bacon hocks, split
2 lb (900 g) beef bones

1 carrot, diced
1 parsnip, diced
1 tablespoon chopped parsley
1 bayleaf
1 medium clove garlic, chopped
2 hard-boiled eggs
3 fl oz (85 ml) dry sherry
Pepper and salt

Leave the beans to soak in water overnight.

Drain the beans the following day and wash well under running water. Place them in a large, heavy-duty casserole, add 3 pints (1.7 l) of water, heat and simmer for about 1½ hours. Stir occasionally and add more water if required.

Remove rind from the bacon, discard and chop into small segments. Peel the onion and chop, together with the celery, into ½" cubes. Fry all these ingredients in the oil until the onion has turned golden but not brown. Remove from the heat and stir in the flour.

When the beans are ready add the frying pan ingredients, bacon hocks, beef bones, diced carrot and parsnip, parsley, bayleaf and garlic to the casserole. Season with about four turns of a pepper mill, return to the heat and bring to the boil. Cover and simmer for about 3–4 hours. Add a little more water during cooking if necessary.

Remove from the heat, discard the bones and bayleaf and pass the soup through a fine sieve or purée in a liquidiser.

Chop the eggs and place them in a small bowl for adding when the soup is served. Re-heat the soup, stir in the sherry and season with salt and pepper before serving.

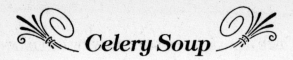

Celery Soup

You entered a different world as you went through the door of the Gay Hussar when Victor presided over it before his retirement. Whatever he was engaged in — phone call, taking an order, seating an attractive girl with obvious relish — whether facing the entrance or with his back to it, he invariably and uncannily noticed the new arrival. 'Lord Balogh!' he would shout directions from the other end, 'Upstairs!' Or he would boom at an MP: 'Mr So and So, telephone!' Authors, publishers, politicians, journalists — he drew them like a magnet. His food was out of this world, though you couldn't count on eating what you had originally planned. Discussion was an illusion. His unmatched powers of persuasion invariably prevailed.

He had spent a few years in the most celebrated kitchen in Budapest before the war, but that doesn't explain how he could speak the impossibly difficult language of Hungarians not only extremely well and colloquially, but also with a slight regional accent. Quite a feat for an Englishman born and bred.

His place was a nostalgic culinary centre for exiled Hungarians, and a refuge — so cheap were his prices. When I first wrote about him in the *Daily Telegraph* in 1952, I commented on his prices: 'Hurry, before he wakes up.' But he never did. His sensuous feel for food was palpable. You were lost the moment he started to explain the high concentration of celery soup (see opposite); the richness of his green beans as an accompaniment for which it would be worth having the main course it came with; the wisdom of ignoring calories in the particular case of plum dumplings. You were putty in his hands and never regretted it.

He once 'guided' me and my diet-conscious lady companion. 'Something light,' she sighed and ended up with a heavy soup, stuffed cabbage and pancakes. We couldn't move, but to our horror Victor bore down on us, after coffee, with two more hefty *main* courses, insisting we should at least taste them. 'It's wonderful,' we both confessed and he reacted triumphantly: 'When you can't eat any more and you still like it, *that's* when food is *really* good!'

CELERY SOUP

Serves 6

1 small bunch white celery, about 1 lb (450g)	1/2 pint (300ml) milk
1 small celeriac, about 10oz (300g)	2 pints (1.1 l) chicken or veal stock
1 small onion	1 heaped teaspoon celery salt
2oz (50g) butter	2oz (50g) lard
1 heaped teaspoon celery seed	2oz (50g) flour
	1/2 teaspoon ground white pepper

For this soup, three saucepans will be in use more or less at the same time, but from start to finish the soup ought not to boil for more than 25 minutes.

Discard one or two of the outside, rough celery sticks and the leaves, to leave about 12oz (350g). Cut this into 1/2" segments. Peel and trim the celeriac to leave about 8oz (225g). Cut into 1/4" slices, then into strips. Peel and slice the onion into thin, quartered rings.

Melt the butter in a large saucepan. Add the onion, celery and celery seed. Stir and cook for 10 minutes. Meanwhile, boil the celeriac in a small saucepan in 1/2 pint (300ml) of the stock. Add the milk and 1 pint (600ml) of the stock to the braising onion and celery. Bring to the boil, add the celery salt and boil for 20 minutes.

Heat the lard in a small saucepan, add the flour and cook over a low heat, while stirring frequently with a wooden spoon, for 8–10 minutes until light brown. Add the remaining stock gradually and beat briskly with a whisk until smooth. (This is not a thickener, but stabilises the soup and gives it the taste and smell of freshly baked bread.)

By now the celeriac will be tender. Liquidise and pour it into the soup and stir. Add the stabiliser (the lard and flour mixture) to the soup, season with pepper, stir well and boil for a further 5 minutes before serving.

Mrs Jókai's Bean Soup

Mrs Jókai, the actress, had two claims to fame: she was the wife of the greatest and most successful Hungarian novelist (in the Thackeray mould) a hundred years ago and her cooking was even more celebrated than her acting. Her villa in the Buda hills across the Danube from Pest was a meeting point for gourmets as well as being a literary salon with a sprinkling of great actors from the National Theatre. In the drive, polished, theatrical carriages mingled with the worn cabs of impecunious writers. I would like to have lived at the *fin de siècle*, so contemporary descriptions of the small crowd arriving at the Jókais fascinate me. Some 50 years later, my parents had a villa near the spot where the Jókais house stood, so I often walked in the garden, thrilled that I was looking at the same unmatched view that must have bewitched all those legendary heroes of my studies.

Mrs Jókai, more used to the stage costumes of tragédiennes, received her guests not in contemporary fineries, but in her apron, making intermittent sorties from the kitchen which only added to the general anticipation. Sunday lunches were a serious business. Often she would herself prepare her husband's favourite soup. Keeping him happy was a vital consideration, not only because Jókai loved his stomach but also because he was some 10 years younger than his wife! Still, it was a very happy marriage and after she died he waited for many years, into his eighties, before marrying again — this time a girl in her twenties!

As far as I know, no aphrodisiac properties are imputed to Mrs Jókai's soup, except an indirect one: from the first spoonful, you can veritably feel a divine fuel in your veins.

MRS JÓKAI'S BEAN SOUP

Serves 6
Preparation starts 24 hours in advance.

About 1¼–1½lb (550–675g)
    smoked knuckle of pork
12oz (350g) dried borlotti beans
    (mostly pink and speckled, also
    known as salugia or crab-eye
    beans)
4 medium carrots
3 medium parsnips
1 large clove garlic
1 sprig of fresh or ½ teaspoon dried
    marjoram

1 bayleaf
5–6 black peppercorns
1 medium onion
2 tablespoons olive oil
¾oz (20g) flour
1 level teaspoon paprika (must be
    'sweet noble' variety)
½ teaspoon vinegar
7–8fl oz (200–225ml) soured cream

Place the meat and beans into a saucepan of cold water to soak overnight.

Next day, clean and cut the carrots and parsnips into ¼″ thick rings. Add these, the crushed clove of garlic, marjoram, bayleaf and peppercorns to the saucepan, but do not salt. Bring to the boil and simmer until meat is quite tender (about 1¼ hours). De-bone the knuckle pork, cut the meat into very small cubes, reserve and keep warm.

Peel and chop the onion. Heat the oil in another saucepan, add the chopped onion and flour and keep stirring until both onion and flour are golden brown. Sprinkle on the paprika, stir once, add a glass of cold water, mix until smooth and add the contents to the saucepan with the beans. Boil for 3–4 minutes, then add the small meat cubes and vinegar.

Before serving, place the soured cream at the bottom of a soup tureen or large casserole, and add the hot soup, *little by little*, while stirring constantly to prevent the cream from curdling.

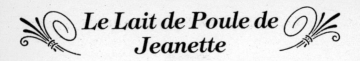

Le Lait de Poule de Jeanette

(The milk of Jeanette's chicken)
at Egon Ronay's Marquee Restaurant, 1953
Chef de Cuisine: Jean Gardes

After a few years as a general manager in two West End restaurants, I decided to go it alone. The old restaurant I took over in Knightsbridge was to take four weeks to refurbish. The builders would work 18 hours a day.

Eight weeks later they were still at it, but the kitchens were ready for a visit by the sanitary inspector, as he used to be called. There was a ground-floor kitchen, but my new pastry kitchen was in the basement. 'You have to change them around,' the inspector said coolly. Simple. We ripped out the kitchen, then the pastry kitchen and started all over again. I lost almost more weight than money. Then some structural fault occurred and the dining room floor had to be taken up. In a rage, I informed the startled builders that I would open in eight days' time, come hell or high water. And I did. The builders worked like images on a video tape when you press the 'fast-forward' button and the customers pirouetted around them.

The third day after I finally got rid of the builders, a woman customer, about to leave, lifted her net shopping bag off a sofa that was covered with a light pink material. It was not the large blood stain that brought me near fainting (there was raw meat at the bottom of her net bag), but the thought of having to re-cover the whole banquette! But that wasn't all: another woman leapt out of her seat, grabbed a large jug of water from a table and emptied it over the sofa. Clearly, the competition wanted to ruin me! Actually, her presence of mind saved the situation and the sofa: the stain eventually disappeared.

It is imprinted on my mind that the culprit had our marvellous soup speciality at the beginning of her bloody lunch.

LE LAIT DE POULE DE JEANETTE

Serves 6

It's worth making a chicken stock for this soup and using the chicken for something else. The use of four chicken stock cubes will be much less effective.

2¼–2½ pints (1.2–1.4 l)
*   de-greased chicken stock,*
*   according to the size of your*
*   6 soup plates or 6 soup cups*
About 10 fresh sorrel leaves

1 oz (25 g) butter
4 egg yolks
2 tablespoons double cream
¼–½ teaspoon salt

De-grease the chicken stock by removing the layer of fat from its top with a paper towel. Bring to the boil.

Wash the sorrel leaves and dry on a paper towel. Cut them into julienne, i.e. into long, very thin pieces with a sharp kitchen knife. Cook them lightly in butter in a frying pan.

Place the egg yolks, double cream and salt into a mixing bowl. Mix thoroughly with a whisk.

Pour the boiling chicken broth into this mixture, then pour back into the saucepan, heat again but do not boil.

Add the julienne of sorrel and serve immediately.

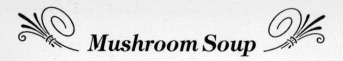

Mushroom Soup

There seems to be a French-inspired convention that it is not correct to serve soup at a dinner party, only at lunch parties. Bunkum. I am a soup addict and like soup as a starting course even at dinner. Not one of the fuller country soups of course — no-one would suggest pasta fagioli for a dinner party. Nevertheless, its flavour should always be self-assertive, except for consommés, which are all the better for being kept very light and delicate and distinguished only by the fragrance of their main ingredient, be it chicken, beef, rabbit or shellfish. (I hesitate to mention, even if only in brackets, that some people consider horse meat best for consommé as it has a sweetish flavour.)

The advantage of consommé is twofold: if you have had strong drinks, such as Martinis, before dinner, it will have a restorative effect on your palate and make it receptive again; and it leaves room for an intermediate course before the main dish. The balance of your fare being all-important, this sequence commends itself, particularly if you serve not only a dessert but also a cheese. I never do so at night unless the main course is unusually light.

However, if your main course is fairly hefty (let us say roast goose with red cabbage), mushroom soup is very appropriate. Though refined, it is flavoursome and just substantial enough to make an intermediate course (before our goose example) superfluous.

The question of croûtons is a controversial one. While — for me — they are enjoyable with much heavier soups (for instance, a pungent fish soup with *rouille*), with such things as mushroom soup I find them a meaningless frill. But I readily bow to differing tastes.

MUSHROOM SOUP

Serves 4

1 lb (450g) button mushrooms
2 oz (50g) stale white bread
Milk (enough to moisten bread)
2 oz (50g) butter
1 medium clove garlic
*2 tablespoons finely chopped
    parsley*

Ground nutmeg
*1 pint (600ml) chicken stock (or 1
    chicken cube dissolved in hot
    water)*
Salt and pepper
4 fl oz (100ml) double cream

Wash the mushrooms under running water and leave to drain. Place the bread in a bowl, pour over a little milk (enough to moisten the bread) and leave to soak. Slice the mushrooms, including the stalks, into small pieces.

Melt the butter in a saucepan and add the mushrooms. Cover and allow to stew gently for 4 minutes, until the mushrooms have softened and yielded some juice. Stir occasionally. Remove from the heat.

Squeeze the surplus milk from the bread. Break the bread into very small pieces and mix into the mushrooms in the saucepan. Finely chop the garlic and add to the saucepan with the parsley, a generous pinch of nutmeg and the chicken stock. Bring to the boil. Lower the heat, cover and simmer gently for 15 minutes. Stir occasionally.

Remove from the heat and leave to cool. Refine in a blender or pass through a sieve. Season with salt and pepper.

Reheat the soup and bring to the boil. Remove from the heat and slowly stir in the cream. Pour into a soup tureen and serve.

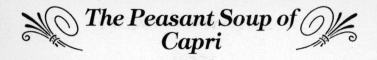 The Peasant Soup of Capri

Since it is so evocative of our beloved Capri, the name of this dish is right, even if Barbara was inspired by the recipe in the book by the late Franco Lagattolla of Mario and Franco fame.

I impute miraculous powers to this wonderful soup for its ability to create an atmosphere of its own, overriding even the English climate. Not a dish that I would serve to our more formal guests (of whom I have mercifully few), but close friends quickly come to appreciate its influence.

On sunny Sundays our guests arrive at noon. There is ritual Champagne which, I am glad to say, no-one wants to spoil by adding anything to it. We eat when the mood takes us and it can happen that at 2.15 p.m. someone makes a remark about getting a bit peckish. We jerk into action while our invaluable Scotsman, Tom Stewart (a fixture at our place in Berkshire and loved by all our friends), pours out what remains of the last bottle of Champagne. Barbara quickly turns a ring on, for this soup has to be served just lukewarm.

Then we sit around the garden table covered with a cloth and laid with innumerable glasses, possibly for a white, a red and a dessert wine. No-one would dream of wearing a tie, and for a few minutes, hunger pangs forgotten, we rave about the superb view of the Berkshire downs rising to the horizon miles away. But among the company of friends, the smell of Barbara's herbs in the rock garden near the table, the view, the ancient, crooked posts flanking the entrance almost hidden by the profusion of clematis and wild roses, something is missing until our largest casserole is placed on the table and the peasant soup of Capri uncovered. For that is, of course, what pulls everything together. Heartfelt exclamations of delight in praise of Barbara. A Mediterranean gathering. Life seems eternal, as in Capri. Miraculous powers, as I said.

THE PEASANT SOUP OF CAPRI

Serves 6

3 large peppers: red, green and
   yellow
2 large courgettes
8 small new potatoes
1 medium onion
3 medium cloves garlic
2 medium carrots
14 oz (397g) tin Italian tomatoes,
   undrained

3 fl oz (85 ml) good olive oil
6 to 8 fresh basil leaves
1 teaspoon dried oregano
Salt and pepper
1 medium aubergine
Additional oil for frying the
   aubergine

Wash, core and de-seed the peppers and cut into rough segments about
1/2" wide. Wash and slice the courgettes into 1/2" rings and scrub the small
potatoes. Peel and cut the onion into fine rings. Finely chop the garlic. Wash
and scrub the carrots and slice them into 1/4" rings.

Place all these ingredients into a large saucepan and add the tinned
tomatoes, roughly chopped, together with the juice. Pour in the olive oil and
season with the basil and oregano. Salt and pepper to taste. Cover the
saucepan, heat and simmer for 30 minutes, stirring the mixture occasionally.

Meanwhile, wash and cut the aubergines into small cubes. Fry in oil
until golden, drain and set aside.

When the vegetables are ready, add the aubergine cubes, mix well,
cover the saucepan and simmer for a further 10 minutes.

Allow to cool, but aim at serving this dish in large soup plates, just warm
enough to appreciate the different vegetable flavours.

Rabbit Consommé

Quick wit, canny repartee, constant cheerfulness and an unfailing capacity to rise to any task — here you have the attractive characteristics of a cockney. Small wonder that when I first came across Brian Turner I thought he must be a cockney; the lack of a cockney accent could be explained away. Subsequently I found out that he is a Yorkshireman and told the story to a friend, who said: 'You should have known — a typical Yorkshireman!' The trouble with that interpretation is that my friend was himself a Yorkshireman.

Be that as it may, it is rare to find a chef-patron who is so much the life and soul of his restaurant — I don't just mean his kitchen, but his comfortable, intimate dining room as well. Now you see him, now you don't. Like a whirlwind, he keeps circling the 40 guests, nips out to the kitchen to adjust a sauce or two — or so you would think, but he is in fact in the vestibule taking a coat, or is he making out a bill? No, he is taking a telephone booking; but he can't be because he is standing at the next table offering advice with a mischievous comment — or is he receiving well-deserved praise for his Chablis? No, no, no: it must have been a mirage, because he is just putting a plate of wonderful *brandade* of sole in front of you. Very confusing.

More importantly, he is a great and inventive cook himself. Witness his tartare of scallops (see page 57), 'sausage' of crab, pear tart with almond paste, and, of course, his perfect consommés. Unless a consommé is perfection itself, for me it is not a consommé at all. I am a very fussy consommé maniac. Dark colour? Forget it: the stockpot has been kept going too long. Slightly salty? The stock was salted a day (or two) before being clarified. Slightly acid taste? The dose of vegetables was too heavy. Bland and empty? Someone has been mean with the meat: trying to get away with bones, or using the cheapest cut, but — foolishly — not shin of beef.

Brian's rabbit-based consommé is clean, its flavour balanced: light and yet with a touch of meat essence about it — for me the essential signs of a perfect consommé.

RABBIT CONSOMMÉ

Serves 6–8

For the rabbit stock
3 rabbit carcasses
6 pints (3.6 l) water
1 leek
4 sticks celery
1 onion
2 carrots
Herbs: parsley stalks, 1 bayleaf,
   juniper berries, sprig of thyme
14 oz (397 g) tin tomatoes

For the consommé
3 rabbit carcasses
1 lb (450 g) large flat mushrooms
1 large carrot
1 large onion
1 leek
1 clove garlic
1 dessertspoon juniper berries
1 teaspoon tomato purée
2 egg whites
Fresh thyme and rosemary
Salt and pepper

Rabbit stock: Put the carcasses into the water, bring to the boil and skim off the scum. Add the vegetables, herbs and tinned tomatoes and simmer for 2–2½ hours. Strain off and allow to cool. This should provide approximately 3 pints (1.7 l) of stock.

Consommé: Chop the rabbit carcasses with a cleaver, mince the mushrooms, carrot, onion, leek and garlic and mix with the juniper berries, tomato purée and egg whites. Stir the mixture thoroughly into the cold rabbit stock.

Bring to the boil and add the thyme and rosemary. Stir frequently until a crust forms. Reduce the heat to a simmer and cook for 1½ hours.

Line a sieve with fine muslin cloth, carefully tip the crust on to the muslin, then strain the consommé through it. Season and garnish according to taste.

Reveller's Soup

A 'house ball' was an intimate affair for 36 to 40 young people, as exciting as the grander balls for 400 or 500 when I was a law student in Budapest before the war. Most of the girls in my wide circle of friends, or rather their mothers, arranged a house ball every season. Because it was very bad form to be on time, we arrived at 9 p.m. though invited for 8, and entered rooms cleared of furniture and Persian carpets to create a dance floor.

The atmosphere was as electric as you can only experience in your twenties. The excitement kept increasing as the pianist sensitively built up the mood, rising to crescendoes of musical numbers as energetic as any today. Behind the civilised exterior of black ties and long, full-skirted dresses of the day, all were caught up in an emotional whirlwind, with well-timed intervals of romantic smooching. Some of us occasionally relieved the exhausted pianist, for dancing was never allowed to stop until 11.30, when the marvellous, candle-lit cold buffet — all of it with an inimitable home-made flavour — was declared open. Ravenous, we destroyed it all in a short time so as to resume dancing, this time a 'csárdás' of unimaginably furious tempo, until, all cheeks paprika-red and some heads spinning, it gave way to a slow waltz or — would you believe it? — a tango as a respite. Sit down? Never!

Pausing only for regular visits to the table for wine, we danced on, many heads slightly swimming now, even though the flow of coffee was endless. Midnight, 1 a.m., 2 — how on earth did we manage it? — then the ritual shouts went up: 'Soup!! Soup!!', as a large, homely soup tureen and a generous supply of lager were carried in. A plate or two of superbly flavoured Reveller's soup restored our powers, cleared our heads and, incredibly, in half an hour we were ready to continue, the poor pianist carried by the sheer momentum of our energy. A party was not a success if guests left before 3 or 4 a.m., and more than once we went straight to lectures or to work after a change of clothes and a quick shave. Those were the days…!

REVELLER'S SOUP

Serves 6

This substantial soup can easily be served as a main course. It is much better when prepared a day in advance and heated up.

2 lb (900 g) tin of sauerkraut
3 oz (75 g) lard (or butter)
3 oz (75 g) flour
1 small onion, very finely chopped
2 heaped teaspoons 'sweet noble' paprika (not the hot variety)
6 rashers smoked bacon (it must be smoked, not green)

Salt and pepper
1½–2 pints (750 ml–1 litre) chicken stock or water
4 frankfurters
⅛ pint (75 ml) soured cream

Squeeze the sauerkraut dry but keep the juice, together with the juice in the tin.

Melt the butter or lard in a large saucepan and stir in the flour. Keep stirring till the roux reaches medium brown colour, add the chopped onion and cook while stirring for another 20–30 seconds, before adding the paprika. Immediately remove from the heat and stir.

Now add the sauerkraut, mix thoroughly and cook, with just enough water to moisten it slightly, for 6–8 minutes. Then add the juice you have kept and all the bacon. Salt and pepper according to taste and top up with chicken stock or water. Cook for about 30 minutes. You can keep this for a day or two (it improves overnight).

Before serving, remove and discard the bacon, bring the soup to the boil. While you do this, boil some water in another saucepan and remove from the heat, then add the frankfurters, cover with the lid and leave for 5–6 minutes. Now cut the frankfurters into rings and add to the soup.

The last touch is adding the soured cream just before serving the soup: place 3 tablespoons of it in a cup, add a ladleful of soup, blend thoroughly into a smooth mixture, stir into the soup and serve.

First Courses

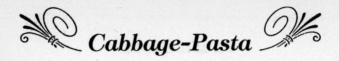

Cabbage-Pasta

Though a 'pasta', it is very substantial and should not be followed by anything heavier than a light grilled fish or veal escalope.

But the situation into which this dish fitted perfectly is not the sort of circumstance you would normally come across. On the Hahnenkamm, 800m above Kitzbühel, in a tiny, 20-room chalet-hotel many miles from everywhere, regulars met Christmas after Christmas for skiing. A spontaneous party was swinging every night in the single, small bar-cum-lounge, the nearest alternative being 45 minutes away by horse-drawn sledge and risky to attempt at night. Spirits rose, fired by copious carafes of Wachauer that would have been harmless in reasonable quantities, and hours after dinner vineous stomachs needed settling. At which point the weaker and the more conventional opted for frankfurters, but the sturdier of us repaired to the kitchen and prepared cabbage-pasta. Enthusiasm often got the better of the amateur cooks, who went over the top with the pepper, creating a vicious circle, as the internal fire only had to be put out by some more Wachauer.

In fact, lager suits cabbage-pasta best in more settled circumstances. It is a fitting meal on a winter evening in any cottage, whether snowbound in the Alps or poured on by the English rain, particularly when it is prefaced by something like a Scotch broth or else followed by a generous piece of farmhouse Stilton, not too ripe, certainly accompanied by some vintage Port, or Banyuls from the South of France, and perhaps a fresh pear.

CABBAGE-PASTA

Serves 4

1 lb 2 oz pasta (500 g) (1″ squares
are best but difficult to obtain
except in some continental
delicatessens, or try to buy fresh
pasta sheets and cut them up. Or
you can use pappardelle, the

wide version of tagliatelle)
1 medium-sized white cabbage
¼ small onion
2 oz (50 g) lard or 3 fl oz (85 ml)
cooking oil
Pepper and salt

Core the cabbage, cut it into six segments, separate and wash the layers; cut out carefully and discard the thickest, white ends. Cut the cabbage into 2″ long pieces. Finely chop the onion.

Heat the fat (or oil) and cook the onion until transparent, but do not let it brown. Add the cabbage to the fat, salt and pepper, and sauté the cabbage, stirring occasionally, until it turns brown. Put aside and keep warm.

Cook the pasta for 5–6 minutes, depending on thickness, if you bought fresh pasta; 7–9 minutes for manufactured pappardelle, again depending on thickness. Strain.

Mix the sautéd cabbage into the pasta and keep cooking and stirring for 2 minutes. Serve on meat plates or large soup plates and grind a little black pepper over it.

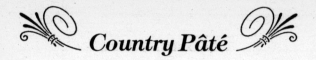

Country Pâté

at Egon Ronay's Marquee Restaurant, 1953
Chef de Cuisine: Jean Gardes

Having spent most of my 22 years as a restaurateur in my father's big establishments, it was daunting to open my own small place in 1952 on a shoestring as a penniless emigré in London. Premises, loans, overdrafts, drinking licence apart, the important thing was to find a brilliant chef. I didn't feel any qualms about pinching one from a fashionable restaurant which I had managed, as I had imported him myself from Beaulieu in the South of France. I duly opened the Marquee, named after its tent-shaped, striped ceiling supported by poles along the walls.

Jean Gardes would now be a celebrated, wealthy chef-proprietor had the British scene been as developed gastronomically as it is today. A most brilliant chef with an artistic touch, he was also a perfectionist. But what really mattered was his unbeatable palate. We were very much ahead of the times and made a good team: I took every order myself, and, having planned the culinary highlights with Monsieur Gardes (we were relentlessly formal), I could sell, with some persuasion, dishes we both thought were best.

Those were barren culinary days, with practically nothing worthwhile in Knightsbridge or Chelsea — everyone headed for Soho and Mayfair. But the Marquee was written up in the *Daily Telegraph* as 'London's most food-perfect small restaurant' and people flocked to taste the rarities unheard of in those days: *pâté de campagne* true to its name (recipe opposite), *matelote d'anguille* smacking of Bordeaux, classic *bouillabaisse* exuding Marseilles, to name a few.

With all that publicity and being opposite the side entrance of Harrods, lunches were particularly hectic. Taking orders, seating the influx, running up and down the stairs to the kitchen and keeping an eye on the waitresses, I was near collapse. A friend of mine, a known wag, watched me and as he was leaving said: 'How much will you pay me if I don't come tomorrow?'

COUNTRY PÂTÉ

Serves 12
This pâté should be prepared 2 days in advance

1½lb (675g) shoulder of pork
1 lb (450g) pork liver
1½lb (675g) lard
4 fl oz (100 ml) dry white wine
3 large shallots, finely chopped
1 medium clove garlic, finely chopped
½ teaspoon finely chopped thyme

2 bayleaves
2 teaspoons finely chopped parsley
2 level teaspoons salt
1 level teaspoon ground black pepper
¼lb (100g) thin pork belly or 8 rashers streaky green bacon (for lining terrine or deep casserole)

Cut the meat and liver into 2–3″ long pieces. Place them with all the ingredients, except the pork belly (or bacon) for lining the dish, into a bowl. Keep the bowl in the refrigerator for at least 12 hours.

Remove the meat and liver, chop roughly with a large kitchen knife, replace in the bowl and mix with the other ingredients.

Line the bottom and sides of a terrine or deep casserole with the pork belly (or bacon). Pour the contents of the bowl into the lined dish and cover with the lid. Place this into a larger dish with hot water in it so that the water comes up to 1″ below the rim of the terrine. Place this so-called *bain marie* in an oven and cook at 180°C (350°F) or gas mark 4 until it is ready: for about 1–1½ hours. You can test if it is cooked by sticking a sharp-pointed, thin utensil (such as a skewer) into the middle of the pâté for 5 seconds, then hold it against your lips: if it feels hot, the pâté is ready.

Remove the dish from the hot water. Place something flat on top of the pâté with a *light* weight to press the pâté and leave it to cool for a few hours. Then put the lid on and keep it in the refrigerator. It should not be started for 2 days and, if refrigerated, it will keep for 6–8 days.

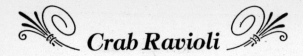

Crab Ravioli

You start lunch at about 2.30 p.m. on the terrace by the side of a vast swimming pool, the only one in Venice: at the Cipriani Hotel. A swim has isolated your skin from the sweltering August heat around the picturesque and odorous narrow canals, far removed from Cipriani's haven. Sunk in a bamboo armchair, you unhurriedly take in the scene and reflect on the irrationality of life: by the time people can afford to stay at the world's most luxurious hotel, most of them are not young enough to take full advantage of the outsize swimming pool which is empty; the 'swimmers', scattered around the pool, lie in a slumber on mattress-covered, white-wood beds with large, soft bath towels.

It has been a full morning since 9 a.m. when the hotel's motor launch (at your beck and call at dawn, dusk or midnight) took you to the San Marco in five minutes. You avoided the 10 o'clock crowds and, for the umpteenth time, followed Hugh Honour's invaluable, well-worn guide to revisit back streets, tiny bridges, your favourite Bellini in an outlying church. The thrill of the day is to discover a detail unchanged since Carpaccio painted it some 500 years ago.

Having immersed yourself in art, you did the same in the pool. (Its size is allegedly the result of a misunderstanding: the financiers' British architects specified feet, but their Italian colleagues understood metres). Now is the time for the shellfish ravioli, followed by grilled *coda di rospo* and a double espresso. Then a leisurely chat with Dr Rusconi who keeps Cipriani at the pinnacle of the world's best hotels.

After the siesta, you swim another few lengths, then take the motor launch to the San Marco and one of the little trattorie, perhaps Da Ivo for a unique *spaghetti al' Gorgonzola*, followed by more espresso at midnight on Florian's terrace in the piazza. You are strangely untroubled by the kitsch music of the orchestra. The Cipriani boat is waiting 200 yards away. You are in love ... with a city.

CRAB RAVIOLI

Serves 6

For the filling
1 small shallot, finely chopped
½oz (15g) butter
3½oz (90g) brown and white
  crabmeat
1 teaspoon brandy
1 egg yolk
1 teaspoon finely chopped parsley
Salt and freshly ground black
  pepper
For the pasta
12oz (350g) semolina
3 eggs
Pinch of salt
1 tablespoon olive oil
1 egg, beaten

**An easier alternative to the
classic sauce**
14oz (397g) can Baxter's cream of
  scampi soup
¼ pint (150ml) double cream
Lemon juice
Salt and freshly ground black
  pepper
For the croûtons
4 slices white bread, crusts
  removed, diced
1oz (25g) butter
2 tablespoons oil
2 cloves garlic, finely chopped
1 tablespoon finely chopped parsley
To decorate
1oz (25g) julienne of carrots
1oz (25g) julienne of courgette

Gently sauté the shallot in butter until it starts to take on colour. Add the crabmeat and moisten with the brandy. Add the egg yolk, finely chopped parsley and season with salt and black pepper.

Ravioli: Mix the semolina, eggs and salt and knead together. Form a ball, lightly cover with oil and let it rest, covered, for ½ hour. Roll the dough very thinly and cut two pieces — 10″ x 10″ and 12″ x 12″. Lightly mark the pasta every 2″ to form squares; place ½ teaspoon of crab mixture on each square. Brush between the crabmeat with beaten egg and place the larger pieces of pasta over the top. Press the dough between each mound of crab. Cut between the squares to give 25 ravioli.

Sauce: Reduce the scampi soup by simmering gently until it measures ½ pint (300 ml). Add the cream, season to taste with lemon juice, salt and black pepper. Keep warm. (*For the classic method:* use a cup of fish stock, 2 cups fresh scampi bisque, a tablespoon each of langoustine butter and brandy, 4 tablespoons mixed white and brown crab meat. Sauté crab meat in butter, add brandy and let it evaporate, add stock and bisque, boil for 2 minutes and thicken with langoustine butter.)

Sauté the diced bread in the butter and oil until brown, add the garlic and cook for 1 minute, then add the parsley and keep warm. Cook the ravioli in boiling water for 5–8 minutes until just soft. Drain and place in a buttered serving dish. Cover with the sauce and decorate with lightly blanched julienne of carrots and courgettes. Serve the croûtons in a separate dish.

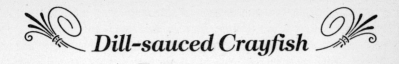

Dill-sauced Crayfish

The most delicate of all shellfish, sweet-river crayfish, must not be used except when it is still alive. The importance of this rule was driven home to me emphatically at a culinary event I arranged some 15 years ago to launch the European section of my guide at Gleneagles.

The lunch was an immense exercise in diplomacy, since I had invited five great chefs from five capitals to prepare a course each. Assigning the courses was no less difficult than casting five prima donnas in the same opera, each one insisting on the main role. With all the persuasion I could command, the menu was finally arranged — and cast. One point no-one could argue: the main course had to be 'given' to a Frenchman, and I cast Claude Deligne, chef de cuisine of Le Taillevent in Paris. I let him choose his main course, wanting to combine all the other courses around it.

He chose chicken and crayfish in an *écrevisse* sauce. I dislike mixing shellfish — or any fish — with meat in the same dish. I pleaded that it would be a risky undertaking to obtain 400 *écrevisses* of good size. 'I will bring them,' he said killing my argument. He brought crates of them the day before the lunch.

I was having tea when an emissary from the kitchens came hot foot with the news that the crayfish were in *extremis*. Disaster! With the decisiveness of a field commander I took action and, with the hotel van, we drove the crates of shellfish, on their last legs so to speak, at great speed to the nearest loch into which they were quickly plunged. We waited anxiously at their crate side. The gods of gastronomy were merciful: the crayfish revived. As far as I could judge, they were happy (the RSPCA would have been proud of me) — though all they had to look forward to was being cooked alive the next day.

Instead of that dish of unhappy memory, I recommend a much better way to prepare *écrevisses*.

DILL-SAUCED CRAYFISH

Serves 4

If crayfish are difficult to obtain, langoustines can be substituted.

For the crayfish
60 small crayfish
1½oz (40g) salt
1 teaspoon caraway seed

Crayfish butter
Crayfish heads (see method)
1 tablespoon oil
1 tablespoon brandy
1 oz (25g) butter

Sauce
1 oz (25g) butter
1 oz (25g) onion, finely chopped
1 oz (25g) flour
¼ pint (150ml) chicken stock
2 heaped tablespoons finely
  chopped dill
Salt and freshly ground black
  pepper
Lemon juice (optional)

Place the salt and caraway seeds into 3 pints (1.7 l) water in a large saucepan, and bring to the boil. Add the live crayfish and boil for 1 minute only. Remove from the heat, add sufficient cold water to reduce the temperature a little (to about 70°C) and let the crayfish cool in the stock. Then remove the crayfish heads, shell the tails and reserve about a third of the heads and the shells for the sauce. Remove the intestines from the tails, clean them and place them in some of the strained stock.

Crayfish butter: Take the reserved heads and shells and crush them in a mortar. Heat the oil in a sauté pan, add the crushed shells and heads and sauté for about 2 minutes on a fairly high heat. Add the brandy and set it alight after 10–15 seconds, then add the butter. Simmer for approximately 10 minutes then strain through a muslin. Keep the crayfish butter warm.

Sauce: Melt the butter in a saucepan and add the chopped onion and flour. Stir over the heat to make a roux without letting it turn brown, add the chicken stock and cook for 20 minutes. Pass through a sieve, then place back on the heat. Add the chopped dill and season with salt and a little freshly ground black pepper. You can add a drop of lemon juice to taste if you wish.

Assembly: Remove the crayfish tails from the stock and add to the sauce. Arrange in a china bowl, sprinkle with the warm crayfish butter and serve with plain rice or steamed, small new potatoes.

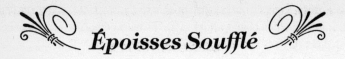

Époisses Soufflé

The modest, self-effacing and youthful Peter Kromberg is, in my considered opinion, among the three or four greatest chefs in the UK. The Soufflé Restaurant at the Intercontinental Hotel, Park Lane, is the home of his original creations, which emerge with unusual frequency and with a total absence of the fanfare and publicity they would richly deserve.

My favourite cheese (this is part of the story) is Époisses, hailing from Burgundy, where it is cured for a few months, then soaked in Marc de Bourgogne for one. To say that it is pungent is a wild understatement: when I bring it home my wife instantly banishes it to my wine cellar (anyway the best place for all cheeses) and, before serving, until the last moment, to the utility room, and even there — she fears — it might give the dirty socks a bad reputation.

When I suggested to Peter Kromberg, on the occasion of an important gastronomic banquet, to try to use Époisses for the cheese soufflé, he took to the idea and, honest man that he is, he now pays me the compliment of calling it 'Soufflé Egon'. Immortality at last! The soufflé is ideally savoury and does not have the somewhat flat taste of ordinary soufflés, including even those made with Parmesan. What is to some people (not to me!) excessive pungency, dissolves into a heavenly aroma you smell the instant the soufflé enters the dining room.

Here are our great chef's hints for soufflés in general: use egg whites a week old and add a pinch of salt to make them stiffer; they stiffen better and more quickly if whipped in a copper bowl; never fill the soufflé dish more than four-fifths; use a plastic spatula for folding the stiff egg whites into the soufflé mixture; make sure that the basic mixture is still hot when you add the stiff egg whites.

But the most important rule is to let the guests wait for the soufflé, never the other way round!

ÉPOISSES SOUFFLÉ

Serves 6

2oz (50g) unsalted butter
1oz (25g) grated Parmesan cheese
1 pint (600ml) milk
1/4 teaspoon nutmeg
Salt and pepper
2 whole eggs
3 egg yolks

3oz (75g) flour
3oz (75g) Gruyère cheese, grated
5oz (150g) Époisses cheese (net
    weight after removing the rind),
    chopped
8 egg whites

Prepare a soufflé dish by buttering it with a quarter of the butter and sprinkle it well with the grated Parmesan cheese.

Pour 3/4 pint (450ml) of the milk into a large saucepan. Add the remaining butter, the nutmeg and season to taste. Bring to the boil.

Mix the 2 whole eggs, 3 egg yolks and the flour into the remaining 1/4 pint (150ml) cold milk and stir this mixture slowly into the boiling milk.

Turn down the heat to very low. When the mixture thickens, remove from the heat and stir in the grated Gruyère and chopped Époisses cheeses. Adjust seasoning, if you think it is necessary.

Whisk the egg whites and fold them gently into the cheese mixture. Pour into the soufflé dish which you have prepared in the way described above. Cook for 30–35 minutes at 170°C (325°F) or gas mark 3.

You may prefer to prepare the soufflé in individual ramekin dishes. If so, the cooking time will only be 15 minutes, but the oven will have to be at 190°C (375°F) or gas mark 5.

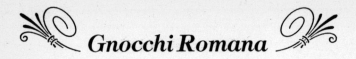

Gnocchi Romana

I arrived fresh from my native country in 1946 and he, a Neapolitan, arrived fresh from a British camp for Italian prisoners. A few months later, one of those odd coincidences that govern life threw us together in a restaurant (now Tramp, a trendy discothèque) in Jermyn Street, a stone's throw from Piccadilly Circus. He was a commis waiter and I the general manager. Mario — whose family name, Cassandro, I only learned a few years later — eventually graduated from the Mirabelle and burst upon the London restaurant scene with a revolutionary trattoria in Soho, The Terrazza, opened on a shoestring, a trend-setter that transformed over night the English perception of eating out. So we were thrown together again in the 1950s: he the innovator, I the dining-out columnist of the *Daily Telegraph*. He whirlwinded around the tables, taking orders, cracking jokes in halting English, conquering stage and film stars with his irrepressible Neapolitan smile, climbing a chair when you ordered grapes to snip a bunch off the vines hanging from the ceiling, which he had appended before the lunch service. And I, fascinated by the Anglo-Neapolitan scene, tried in vain to assess his unique place objectively for a write-up. We have been close friends ever since.

After going 'public' he became a millionaire and retired to Italy, but his heart brought him back to England and to restaurants. He now owns the most attractive and tasteful Mario's in South Kensington, London, is as active as ever on entering his seventies and — there is hope for us all — he continues chasing the girls.

But back to gastronomy. Gnocchi Romana, my favourite pasta (if it can be called a 'pasta'), which I often have at Mario's, is usually prepared in layers the way Mario prescribes in his recipe on the page opposite. However, I also like it in individual portions, the shape and size of a very small, upturned ramekin dish: three on a plate, surrounded by a small amount of light-coloured breadcrumbs very lightly fried in half butter and half oil, but kept almost as loosely textured as a sauce.

GNOCCHI ROMANA

Serves 6

2 egg yolks
³/₄ pint (450 ml) milk
Chicken stock cube (optional)
¹/₂ lb (225 g) semolina

Salt
6 oz (175 g) grated Parmesan cheese
4 oz (100 g) unsalted butter

Beat the egg yolks. Boil the milk in a saucepan. A chicken stock cube can be added to the milk (optional). Add the semolina in a steady stream while stirring energetically with a wooden spoon so that lumps do not form. Continue stirring for 10 minutes until the mixture thickens.

Remove from the heat, add salt, the beaten egg yolks, half the Parmesan and half the butter. Continue stirring until all the ingredients are blended.

Pour the mixture on to a flat, damp surface, wet a large knife and spread the mixture evenly to a thickness of 1¹/₄″. Let it cool, then cut with a round cutter into shapes of about 2″ diameter. Arrange these in a buttered baking tray or at the bottom of a buttered, shallow dish, so that the cut out shapes slightly overlap each other. Sprinkle the remaining grated Parmesan on top and dot with the remaining butter.

Bake at 225°C (425°F) or gas mark 7. Serve hot.

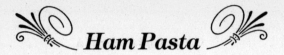

Ham Pasta

Nations are very possessive about pasta. Consider, for example, the Chinese, who are supposed to have invented it (I wonder how such theories find their way into serious reference books). There are a few Chinese chefs who can perform a riveting cabaret act by turning a flat sheet of pasta into thin spaghetti shapes within two minutes without using any utensil. They keep folding the pastry and throwing it forcefully onto a table, simultaneously twisting and turning it. Pasta is a Chinese thing, they would say. The French, though apt to make deprecating remarks about macaroni and other pasta when they characterise Italian cooking, use it with surprising frequency, though admittedly their pasta is much thinner and more delicate. There are numerous French dishes sauced in such a way that pasta, usually light, thin tagliatelle, becomes more than an accompaniment — it almost makes the dish. And who would doubt the glory of lightly sauced, paper-thin ravioli filled with pieces of some shellfish or other?

I don't have to say anything about Italians, except that to dispute, to their faces, Italian superiority in this field is asking for trouble.

Now the role of pasta in Central European cooking is different. The many delicious, substantial pasta dishes are not served as a first course, as they are in Italy. They are either main courses or eaten at the end of the meal. Unusual, too, is the sweet variety: you would miss a habit-forming experience if you didn't try them.

The problem about ham pasta is that pasta squares are by far the best thing for it. Would you believe that such a shape does not exist in the normal, incredibly varied Italian repertoire? Imported from other countries, it is usually available in delicatessens. Next best thing is to buy freshly made flat sheets and cut them up, though these might not be thin enough. Dare I suggest that you make your own?

HAM PASTA

Serves 6
This substantial dish could also be served as a main course.

³/₄lb (350g) square pasta. Ideal are 1″ squares, but difficult to get. Worth the trouble of making them fresh. Next best is medium-sized farfalle (shaped like a bow tie)
¹/₂lb (225g) smoked rashers streaky bacon

2 tablespoons cooking oil
3oz (75g) butter, softened
Salt
1 egg yolk
³/₄ pint (450ml) soured cream
¹/₂lb (225g) lean, minced ham
1oz (25g) grated Parmesan cheese

Cut the bacon rashers into ¹/₂″ squares. Fry in one tablespoon of the oil in a saucepan until it starts getting crisp, but do not crisp entirely. Butter a shallow casserole and pre-heat the oven to 225°C (425°F) or gas mark 7.

Cook the pasta in salted water, adding a spoonful of oil to prevent sticking. For cooking time, follow the instructions on the packet. For freshly made pasta: 3–4 minutes if the pasta is thin.

Beat the egg yolk and mix into the soured cream. Add the minced ham and fried bacon pieces. Add this mixture and the remainder of the softened butter to the drained pasta and mix thoroughly so the ingredients are evenly distributed. Pour this into the casserole and sprinkle with grated cheese.

Cook in the oven for 30 minutes. Bring the casserole to the table and serve by cutting squares with a sharp knife and lifting them out with a palette.

A green salad with vinaigrette dressing can accompany it profitably.

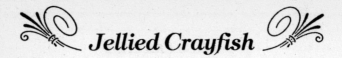

Jellied Crayfish

Sweet-river crayfish is the most delicate and most underestimated of all shellfish. All its sea-water relatives have a more assertive flavour, but crayfish are best when eaten unembellished or perhaps with some sympathetic, low-key sauce. I have a soft spot for these river relatives when they are made to swim again after they have been cooked: served *à la nage* i.e. 'swimming' in a minimally flavoured butter sauce which lets their natural flavour shine.

Sweet-river crayfish are used in many combinations, but I also love them plain boiled: after having twisted and extracted the middle scale of their tail with their gut adhering to it, you cook them alive. This looks more horrid in black and white than it is in action. All you add to the fiercely boiling water is sea salt and caraway seeds — fiercely boiling for culinary reasons and also because this instantly anaesthetises and kills the fish. (You often have to swallow your sensitivities before swallowing a delicious preparation.) Plain, boiled crayfish will not stand up to any other flavour, except perhaps that of unsalted butter. However, you do have to find specimens of reasonable size, with a tail at least $1^{1}/_{4}$ to $1^{1}/_{2}''$ long. The majority on the market are tiny and are not only flavourless but also have such miniature claws that the flesh — if you succeed in extracting it at all — is no bigger than a small pea. Quite useless.

Being characterless, crayfish lend themselves to all manner of chefs' creative urges when they enter the fantasy world of *nouvelle cuisine*. This is where originality counts, provided it is coupled with good taste.

Chef Peter Kromberg has both in abundance. Hence his creation of what has become one of my favourite dishes. When I think of booking a table two to three days in advance at the fabulous Soufflé Restaurant at the Intercontinental Hotel in Park Lane, I try to ring him first to see whether he can obtain the crayfish to make this wonderful first course.

JELLIED CRAYFISH

Serves 6

If crayfish are difficult to obtain, langoustines can be substituted.

36 medium-sized, fresh-water, live crayfish

2 tablespoons white wine vinegar

1 bouquet garni

1 medium onion, studded with cloves

1 bayleaf

5 pints (2.85 l) seasoned chicken stock (made with 2–3 chicken cubes)

3 medium artichokes

2 tablespoons fresh lemon juice

2 fl oz (60 ml) vinaigrette dressing (see page 53)

2 fl oz (60 ml) cocktail sauce or mild vinaigrette dressing

6 thin slices goose liver pâté

6 poached quail's eggs

2 leaves gelatine

1 small bunch tarragon

Salt, pepper

Cayenne pepper

2 bunches watercress

Cut six strips of very thin cardboard 2″ wide and 8″ long. Shape them into rings, staple fast and set on a tray.

Add the vinegar, bouquet garni, the studded onion and bayleaf to the chicken stock and bring to the boil. Add the live crayfish and bring back to the boil. Remove the crayfish, break off their heads, shell and de-vein the tails, and return the heads to what is now a boiling court bouillon. Cook for a further 5 minutes.

Cook the artichokes in water flavoured with the lemon juice until tender. Cool, then break off the leaves so that only the bottoms are left. Remove the hairs and cut into thin slices. Mix with the vinaigrette dressing and place into the bottom of the paper rings.

Trim the crayfish tails neatly, mix the trimmings with the cocktail sauce or a mild-flavoured vinaigrette dressing, and place them on top of the artichoke salad layers. Add thin slices of goose liver pâté on top. Arrange six crayfish tails in a neat, circular pattern on top of the goose liver slices and place a poached quail's egg in the centres of your patterns.

Soak the gelatine leaves. Chop the tarragon stalks and the leaves separately. Bring the court bouillon to the boil, add the chopped tarragon *stalks* and soaked gelatine and season with salt and freshly ground black pepper. Sprinkle on a pinch of cayenne pepper and strain into a bowl. Stand this, surrounded by ice cubes, in a bigger bowl and stir until cold. When the jelly starts to thicken, add the chopped tarragon *leaves* and pour into the rings, just enough to cover the poached quail's eggs and crayfish tails. Leave in the refrigerator for 3 hours.

With the help of a spatula, place the solidified rings on dessert plates and carefully remove the cardboard rings. Serve with a very small amount of watercress salad.

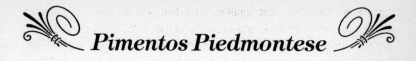

Pimentos Piedmontese

It is ridiculous to force food into the straitjacket of nationalities, races and countries, to erect rigid language barriers on menus. It contradicts the universality of the palate. This bogus stance could only develop because most customers and too many restaurateurs are insecure in their judgement and clutch at the absurd conventions of food snobbery. This is why we get restaurants with exclusively British staff using French on menus and in the kitchen; why we are arrogantly told what is 'correct' and what is 'wrong' in combining food, or what you must drink with what. You can *advise* people what they might enjoy and may wish to try, but no 'rules' please. The only criterion is what you actually fancy.

The true internationality of food is enshrined in Simon Hopkinson's kitchen practice and menu at the Bibendum restaurant in Fulham Road, London. He really doesn't give a fig for conventions and indulges in what he likes and what he thinks his customers will love. His risotto is most Italian, his chicken dish very English and the foie gras (one of London's best) couldn't be more French. His menuese, too, is what customers understand, written in mixed language, not of the *le porridge au lait* school.

The acquisition of the fascinating *fin de siècle* Michelin building, housing Bibendum, wasn't Sir Terence Conran's main coup; nor was it the Michelin company's astonishing permission to use its emblem, the tyre man, on menus and in decor. It was the capture of chef-partner Simon Hopkinson, whose down-to-earth, anti-snob approach to food is the best news on the catering scene for a long time. May he set a trend.

When you follow the recipe overleaf and indulge in his richly flavoured, softly textured, picturesque pimentos *Piedmontese* (which he rightly describes in Anglo-Italian), what do you care about abstract purity?

PIMENTOS PIEDMONTESE

Serves 4

2 large red peppers
2 large ripe tomatoes (they must be ripe)
2 cloves garlic

Pepper and salt
Virgin olive oil (a good quality oil is essential for flavour)
8 anchovy fillets

Split the peppers in two lengthwise. Discard the membrane and seeds. Skin the tomatoes and cut in half. Slice the garlic into thin slivers.

Divide the garlic between the four pepper halves. Cover with the four halved tomatoes, rounded side uppermost. Liberally grind pepper all over and sprinkle with a little salt.

Put the peppers into an ovenproof dish and generously pour over the virgin olive oil.

Pre-heat the oven to 190°C (375°F) or gas mark 5 and roast for about 1 hour or until the edges of the peppers are slightly scorched.

Leave until lukewarm and arrange the anchovies in a criss-cross fashion over each pepper before serving.

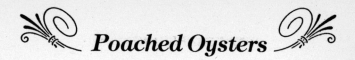

Poached Oysters

The saying goes that the most courageous man ever was the one who first dared to eat an oyster. At any rate he must have been the hungriest. He must also have been canny to divine the gastronomic treasure locked within the armour, or he may have been simply after a pearl and fancied a snack between dives.

The two camps, eaters and non-eaters of oysters (swallowers would be more apt), are firmly divided, and I suspect that the negative camp is more numerous. Yet they seem to be shy about their inclination, as if it were some allergy, and when the moment of truth arrives, there is invariably an undertone of apology when they refuse oysters. Perhaps they have an oyster complex, or possibly feel envy towards those who live a fuller gastronomic life? By the way, we may all have become culinary sissies, considering that our great-grandparents used to eat many dozens at one sitting by way of a snack.

Not that the positive camp is undivided. I may be stepping on culinary sensibilities, but I do feel that the addicts of large, fat specimens are not discerning oyster eaters. Large Whitstables put me off — I am a staunch Helford man. It was the uncrowned king of oystermen, the late Bill Bentley, who warned me a long time ago to squeeze a little lemon on them, not only for taste but also to ensure none were dead — if they cringe, they are alive.

If poached oysters are prepared as they should be, they are almost uncooked, and there are few dishes more sensuous and refined. Now Marco Pierre White's are unforgettable (the recipe is overleaf), and so are many of his other dishes, quite something for a chef-patron in his twenties! He only burst on the scene some two years ago but rose like a rocket. Demonically mercurial, young, riveting to watch on the screen, he achieved well-deserved fame and success at Harvey's in Wandsworth in an improbably short time.

POACHED OYSTERS

Serves 4

Basic pasta
1 lb 2 oz (500 g) plain flour
½ teaspoon salt
1 teaspoon olive oil
4 eggs
6 egg yolks
1 oz (25 g) butter (for warming
  through)
Main ingredient
20 oysters (opened and their juice
  retained and rounded shells kept
  for serving)

Sauce Beurre Blanc
4 shallots chopped very, very finely
3 fl oz (85 ml) white wine vinegar
8 oz (225 g) unsalted butter
Salt and pepper
Lemon juice
Garnish
4 oz (100 g) dark green cucumber
Butter (see method)
Fresh seaweed or rock salt
2 tablespoons caviar

For the pasta: Put the flour, salt and ½ teaspoon olive oil in a mixer and process for a few seconds. Add the eggs and yolks and mix until the pasta begins to come together. Knead the pasta well on a flat surface until the mixture is even and smooth. Cut into eight pieces, wrap each ball in clingfilm and allow to rest in the refrigerator for 20 minutes.

Roll the pasta out very thinly and cut into fine strips. Cook in boiling salted water for 30 seconds. Refresh in cold water, drain and then toss in the remaining drops of olive oil. Set aside.

For the sauce: Put the finely chopped shallots in a pan with the vinegar and boil to remove the acidity and concentrate the flavours. Add a little water and bring back to the boil. Remove the pan from the heat and gently but quickly whisk in the butter piece by piece. Leave the sauce for 20 minutes for the shallots to infuse. Season with salt and pepper and perhaps a little lemon juice and then pass through muslin cloth. Check for taste again, and keep warm.

To assemble: Wash the rounded oyster shells, cover them with water in a pan and bring to the boil (which will both clean and warm the shells). Poach the oysters in their own juices (which have been strained to remove any traces of shell) until just firm to the touch — about $1\frac{1}{2}$ minutes. In another pan, gently warm the pasta through with a little butter and water and season.

Peel and seed the cucumber and cut into julienne strips ($1\frac{1}{2}''$ long). Cook in just enough water to cover and add a little butter. The julienne strips should not be too wet.

To serve: Dress each plate with seaweed or rock salt and place the five oyster shells on the plate securely. Wind the pasta round a fork to make a little nest to settle in the base of each shell. Place an oyster on top. Top with a few cucumber strips. Spoon the beurre blanc gently over the oyster and top each oyster with a little of the caviar.

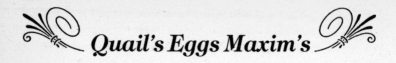

Quail's Eggs Maxim's

The Shah of Iran arranged a megalomaniac feast for the 2,500th anniversary of his country. The logistics defied the most vivid imagination. In the absence of suitable buildings at the site of the historical processions, hundreds of improvised dining rooms were created in the form of most luxurious silk tents furnished as if they were royal palaces. Indeed, they were occupied by royalty and heads of state from all over the world. The main objective was an unmatched PR exercise. The big problem, particularly for the very top échelons of guests, was the food.

To provide for the considerable number of illustrious guests, the Shah's organisers turned to Chez Maxim's in Paris. Its proprietor, the late Louis Vaudable, showed me details, including unimaginably elaborate menus made of silk and precious wood. A small army conscripted from the cream of Parisian chefs was flown to Iran.

The first course, not surprisingly, was made with Persian caviar used in an original way. It was so successful that the dish became a classic, something that only happens on those exceedingly rare occasions when the invented dish is imitated, then accepted by popular vote, and finally finds its way onto menus everywhere. The process takes many years.

The price of caviar would have made it difficult for the original version of Quail's Eggs Maxim's to become a classic; the second version, which did so, had also been developed by Maxim's and was a master stroke. As you can see from the recipe, it consists of a small boat-shaped pastry case with a bed of caviar on which three (or two) poached quail's eggs are placed and covered with Hollandaise sauce. The ingenious second version replaced the caviar with mushroom purée. It is delicious and relatively easy to make. And for a very special occasion it is even worth making the original version.

QUAIL'S EGGS MAXIM'S

Serves 4

1 lb (450g) mushrooms
3 oz (75g) butter
Lemon juice
Salt and pepper
16 raw quail's eggs
1 tablespoon vinegar
4 small puff-pastry cases, boat
shaped (approximately 10 cms
diameter)

Hollandaise sauce
2 egg yolks
5 oz (150g) unsalted butter, melted
Salt
1/2 teaspoon lemon juice

Finely mince the mushrooms and fry them in the butter with lemon juice. Season with salt and a little freshly ground black pepper.

Poach the eggs in simmering water with a little vinegar, for 1 minute. Take them out and drain on a piece of cloth.

Gently heat the cases in a warm oven, stuff with the minced mushrooms and place the eggs on top. Cover with the Hollandaise sauce and serve hot.

(To make the Hollandaise sauce, take the egg yolks, add a tablespoon of water and whip in a bain marie to a ribbon stage. Remove the bain marie from the heat and whip the eggs for a further 10 seconds. Slowly and gradually add the melted butter, but not the sediment, and season with a pinch of salt and the lemon juice.)

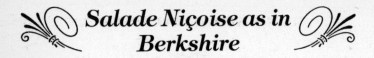

Salade Niçoise as in Berkshire

The exciting and absorbing thing about cooking is the scope it gives for varying a dish and for experimenting. Every region, every family, has its ways with *coq au vin*, and a *cassoulet's* contents can be a delightful surprise. *Salade Niçoise* is another example. There are prigs who will lecture you about the sacrilege of leaving out French beans or adding spring onions. I add herbs liberally, depending on what is in its prime in the garden — and to hell with the classic recipe.

Let me share with you an intriguing story I have never told anyone, intriguing not because of what happened, but because it has been treated by its two protagonists (I was one) as if it had never happened.

One evening soon after I opened my Marquee restaurant in Knightsbridge in the early 50s, an early diner came and I took his order. The young man, probably in his early twenties, ordered *salade Niçoise*, which even my Southern French chef, a master of this dish, served without garlic unless it was asked for. As the diner was leaving, I courteously inquired whether he was satisfied. He asked: 'Don't you *ever* serve *salade Niçoise* with garlic?' in a tone of voice that eventually became his hallmark. It put my back up and — unforgivably for a restaurateur — I turned on the young man: 'You have a lot to learn!' (I remember my words very clearly). He fired back, 'So have you!' and left in a huff. I have met Sir Clement Freud, as he now is, dozens of times over the years and am a sincere admirer of his wit as well as his great gastronomic knowledge, but we have never acknowledged our first encounter and I have never told anyone — until now. Perhaps it is not too late to apologise some 36 years on. I wonder whether he remembers?

SALADE NIÇOISE AS IN BERKSHIRE

Serves 6

¼lb (100g) French beans (they
    must be thin)
1½ x 7oz (198g) tins tuna fish
3 round lettuces
1 chicory (French endive)
1 red pepper
2 sprigs dill
1 sprig tarragon
1 small bunch chives
15 anchovy fillets

20 black olives (preferably stoned
    Kalamata olives)
For the vinaigrette dressing
1½ tablespoons sherry vinegar (or
    other wine vinegar)
2 pinches salt
Freshly ground black pepper (three
    turns of the pepper mill)
1 teaspoon Dijon mustard
2 medium cloves garlic
3½ tablespoons olive oil

Top and tail the French beans, boil them for 1½ minutes, drain and leave them to cool. Break up the tuna fish with a fork into 1″ chunks. Discard the outer leaves of the lettuce, separate and wash the rest of the leaves then dry them by very gently pressing them between two kitchen cloths or paper towels. Top and tail the endive, separate the leaf layers, wash and dry them in the same way. Cut the core out of the red pepper, rinse it with fast-flowing water from the tap to get rid of the pips and cut into ⅛″ thick rings. Wash and dry the dill, tarragon and chives, then chop them but not too finely.

Line a very large — preferably shallow — salad bowl with the lettuce leaves. Then distribute the rest of the vegetables over them, followed by the anchovy fillets, tuna fish chunks and black olives. Sprinkle with all the chopped herbs.

Make the dressing immediately before serving: pour the vinegar into a small bowl, add the salt, pepper and mustard. Peel the cloves of garlic and squeeze them through a garlic press into the vinegar. Pour the olive oil gradually into the bowl while mixing it forcefully with a small whisk. Pour the dressing on to the salad and, at the table, mix the dressing thoroughly into the salad.

Sautéd Cottage Pasta

The Mátyás Pince (Mathias Cellar), one of Budapest's oldest and largest brasseries — with a sloping floor, tables surrounded by boxes and wood panelling with a warm, red–brown patina — was a favourite peace-making venue after duels.

I speak from experience. Someone had made a stupid but offensive remark about the social standing and family background of my closest friend and me (we were both 20). The code of our circle was merciless: there had to be a duel. Our seconds chose the weapons, pistols, the venue and the time: the woods at 5 a.m. My friend and I drew lots: my friend lost, so he would fight for both of us. Our 'duel doctor' warned him to fast for 12 hours — if he was shot in the stomach, an operation would be less messy.

I fetched him, our seconds and our doctor. A brand new driver with a brand new car on roads frozen like ice rinks, and, with frayed nerves, I collided with a lorry on the way to the woods. The others went on by taxi. Eventually, I followed them and met an ambulance, speeding from the woods, siren screaming. My friend was the apple of his father's eye and the duel had, of course, been kept a deep secret. How was I going to face his family? How would I tell my father about the duel and the wrecked car?

But it was a false alarm. Neither of the duellists had been hurt. The pistols, like something out of an Errol Flynn film, had long barrels and were not as accurate as modern guns.

Straight after the duel, the code prescribed, it had to be drinks with your intended killer, so we repaired to the Mathias Cellar for copious breakfast and beer to calm stomachs and nerves.

The minute matriarch of the family-run brasserie, always in black with a cloth apron, used to visit every table to inquire, with a charming little curtsey and a diffident smile, how everything had been. The food is still outstanding, and the wonderful pasta dish they served me brought back the memories of that duel long ago.

SAUTÉD COTTAGE PASTA

Serves 6

1½lb (675g) semolina
4 eggs, beaten
Salt
2½oz (65g) lard
Semolina for working the dough

5oz (150g) smoked bacon, finely
  chopped
½ pint (300ml) soured cream
1lb 6oz (625g) cottage cheese

Sift the semolina through a fine wire-mesh, drum-shaped sieve. Mix the sieved semolina with the eggs and salt and knead the mixture with enough water so as not to make the dough too soft, i.e. it should be on the harder rather than the softer side. Cut the dough into 3 or 4 pieces and knead each again thoroughly. Form them into round bread shapes, lightly grease by hand with 2oz (50g) of the lard and cover with a kitchen cloth. Rest them for 15 minutes.

Stretch each piece of dough with a rolling pin, on a surface dusted with semolina, into *thin* sheets. Sprinkle the sheets very lightly with semolina and leave them to settle for 4–5 minutes.

Place the finely chopped bacon in a large saucepan. Sauté on a hot ring until its fat has been rendered and tiny, crisp bacon pieces are formed.

Boil lightly salted water in a large saucepan and add the remaining ½oz (15g) lard to prevent the pasta from sticking. Tear each pasta sheet into pieces of about 1¼–1½″ square, sprinkle them very lightly with flour and spread them into a single layer if there is room. Place the pieces in the boiling water. When they surface and are cooked, fish them out with a strainer, allow them to drain and then rinse them thoroughly.

Add the cooked pasta to the saucepan containing the bacon fat and crisp bits. Mix thoroughly. Sauté this mixture on a very hot ring, while stirring occasionally, until the pasta gets slightly crispy. While doing so, salt sparingly (to taste) if necessary.

Meanwhile, slightly warm the soured cream (not too much). Crumble the cottage cheese into pieces as small as you can, and warm in a low, open oven.

Dish out the pasta on large plates, heap some cottage cheese on each and pour the warm soured cream over the heap.

Scallops Tartare

The vogue of Japanese cooking probably stems from the sadly growing fad of ascetic food, mainly as a result of the current obsession with health. As for the fundamentalists, the leaf-munching meat haters — we should have understanding and respect for all religions, but I do feel sorry for such retarded gastronomes with carrot juice flowing through their veins.

I am not an admirer of Japanese food in general. As for raw fish — God knows, I have tried hard and experimented many times to understand its allure, but remain unpersuaded — except, of course, for oysters, though I am baffled by people who love the very big, fat, sickly size. But the small variety, for example the marvellous Helford oysters, are a treat.

Nevertheless, there are two raw fish dishes to which I am addicted. One, as far as I know, was first served by Raymond Blanc: salmon tartare. The other is Brian Turner's dish (he is chef-patron of Turner's Restaurant in Walton Street, Chelsea). I was taken aback when he explained that it consists of raw scallops but I never regretted my courage.

It's the ideas that count and Brian Turner is full of them. He is a good example of how important intelligence and sensitivity are in culinary matters. There is no such thing as an insensitive, unintelligent great cook. The same applies to the appreciation of food in general and a good palate. This is not to say that *all* intelligent and sensitive people have a good palate! But it is certainly true that those who do have it are usually intelligent and sensitive.

SCALLOPS TARTARE

Serves 4

2 small shallots
12 midget gherkins
16 whites of scallops
2–3 teaspoons fresh lemon juice
2–3 teaspoons olive oil
Salt and pepper

Selection of salad leaves according
*   to taste such as curly endives,*
*   radicchio, young spinach leaves,*
*   lambs lettuce or roquette*
Salad Niçoise recipe (page 53)

Chop shallots very finely. Cut the gherkins into julienne (the thinnest possible) strips with a large, sharp kitchen knife.

Cut the whites of scallops into fine dice. The natural freshness of the scallops will make the whole cling together.

Mix the scallops, gherkins and shallots together in a bowl, season with lemon juice, olive oil, salt and pepper.

Shape the mixture in the centre of a plate using a circular mould. Season the selection of salad leaves with a little vinaigrette dressing and surround the scallop tartare with them.

Skate Salad

It is not only refinement that the words 'French cuisine' imply, but mostly a complicated cooking process. So when experts in France praise a dish, they may well emphasise that it has succeeded (*c'est bien réussi*). Beyond the flavours and textures, one is delighted to recognise the mastery of the skill the preparation reflects. If it all clicks, it's a *tour de force.*

I am full of admiration for the experience and professionalism all this demands. But culinary acrobatics do not have a monopoly of the palate. It is a hackneyed truth that the result of simple cooking can be just as delicious if the raw materials are excellent, or that some basic foods, without anything being done to them, give just as much pleasure as involved French cuisine. I carry on and on about the marvels of a light and well-flavoured Yorkshire pudding, but who would deny that there is something awesomely clever, for example, in a toothsome terrine of woodcock?

The surprising thing about John Burton-Race, chef-patron of l'Ortolan at Shinfield, Reading, is that many of his dishes go beyond even these achievements. Almost without exception, his cooking is so complicated that one suspects it springs from masochism. The results can be uncanny because the innumerable constituents of a single dish are chosen with such intuition that they may create a single, harmonious flavour. It all shows a sense of balance and judgement exceptional in a man of 32. The psychological reasons for his self-torturing performances are difficult to fathom, but basically they are a burning, obsessive desire to do things well, and imagination evidenced by the unusual nature of his combinations. These attributes are also brought to bear on a few simpler dishes that wouldn't necessarily defeat a non-professional cook. Not to prejudice my appetite before one of his creations, I sometimes ask for a simple skate salad which you will not find difficult to prepare at home.

SKATE SALAD

Serves 4

2 x 1¼lb skate wings (outer fins removed and washed)
2oz (50g) melted butter, flavoured with garlic, lemon, cayenne and chopped blanched tarragon
2 medium carrots and 2 medium courgettes cut into julienne
Salt and freshly ground black pepper
½ pint (300ml) fish consommé or clear fish stock
Vinaigrette dressing (see page 53)

1 teaspoon finely chopped tarragon
2 finely chopped shallots
1 bunch chives
Soya sauce
4oz (100g) baby spinach leaves (pousses d'epinard)
4oz (100g) roquette
6oz (175g) yellow frizzy (curly endive)
Lemon juice
2 blanched, skinned then diced tomatoes

To steam the skate: Lay the skate on thick, heat-resistant, plastic film wrap (such as Clingo-Wrap) or microwave wrap. Brush it with the flavoured butter, sprinkle with the julienne of vegetables and lightly season with salt and pepper. Place the skate wings on top, brush them with the same butter and seal. The parcels must be completely airtight.

Steam for five minutes on each side or until tender, take out and leave to cool. Unwrap. Save the julienne to use in the salad and strain off the cooking juices and save for the sauce then skin and fillet the skate. Keep warm and covered to retain the moisture.

For the sauce: Mix together the cooking juices and the fish consommé (or clear fish stock). Reduce the liquid by half, strain and cool. Combine the vinaigrette dressing with the chopped tarragon and whisk in one tablespoonful to enrich the sauce. Finish with chopped shallots and chives, but reserve two teaspoons of each for the salad. Add the soya sauce and correct the seasoning.

For the salad: Wash and dry the salad leaves. In a bowl mix the leaves with the reserved shallots and chives, add the tarragon vinaigrette and a few drops of soya sauce. Check seasoning.

To assemble: At the last possible moment prepare the salad and arrange on four plates. Place the skate, cut into slices, around the edge of each plate, season it with lemon juice and sprinkle the julienne and diced tomato over it.

Flash through a warm oven for 3 seconds. Spoon the sauce over the skate and serve.

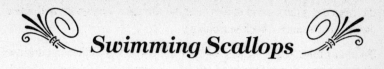

Swimming Scallops

Some 16 years ago I surveyed and graded, together with my senior inspector, the 32 top restaurants in Paris for my guide. We disagreed with a number of the Guide Michelin's star ratings, dramatically so with a few, and I wrote an article for *The Times* about unquestioning British snobbery in adulating French taste and the inadequacy of some highly rated restaurants (one of them was taken out of Michelin altogether the following year). *Paris Match*, in a three-page article, though indignant at the British gall to criticise, agreed with many of our views. I also received a most courteous letter from the President of l'Académie des Gastronomes which, like the Académie Française, has 40 members, inviting me to their next monthly luncheon for a discussion. Breaking with their tradition of the President's assessment of every meal and hoping to show up their British guest, they shocked me: I was unexpectedly asked to assess the meal.

A few things happened to leave room for criticism at that very high level, and I am nothing if not frank in such matters. Needled by the suspect compliment of being asked for my views, and with apologies for being a very outspoken guest, I squashed the venerable members' belief that the British didn't have a gastronomic leg to stand on. I thought that first appearance would be my last, but the French can be surprisingly meek when told a few home truths and the invitation was repeated monthly from then on. They kept testing my reactions for five years. Then a severe winter eased one or two ageing members out of their *fauteuils* for ever and they made an exception to their xenophobic custom by electing me a member.

Apart from the Académie, the Club des Cent, another august gastronomic society, also holds its monthly luncheons Chez Maxim's. On these occasions chef de cuisine Michel Menant rises above the restaurant's current standards. I have, over the years, enjoyed his *Coquilles St Jacques à la nage* more than once. Being intolerant of French menuese, I attempted a translation to popularise what is, to me, one of the highlights of French cooking.

SWIMMING SCALLOPS

Serves 6

30 fresh scallops
4 oz (100 g) carrots, sliced
4 oz (100 g) baby onions, sliced
1 bouquet garni
Salt and pepper

1 pint (600 ml) fish stock
10 oz (300 g) butter, unsalted
Parsley to garnish
1 lemon

Cook the sliced carrots and baby onions in water with a bouquet garni, salt and pepper. When tender, drain and reserve the vegetables.

If the scallops are large, slice them through the middle horizontally. Cook the scallops in the fish stock for approximately 1–2 minutes according to size, and transfer them to a warmed serving dish.

Boil the stock until it is reduced by about one third and add 5 oz (150 g) diced butter, moving the saucepan constantly. Season with salt and pepper as required.

Pour the sauce on the scallops, add the drained vegetables and decorate with sprigs of parsley.

Cream the remaining butter and season with salt, pepper and lemon juice. Serve in a sauce boat.

Fish (main course)

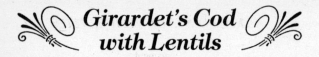

Girardet's Cod with Lentils

Some 12 years ago, I received a postcard from the late proprietor of Chez Maxim's. 'I have found', he wrote from Switzerland, 'the world's best restaurant. I urge you to visit Giradet'. Relevant to this is another story about a businessman friend of mine with an unerring palate and with exceptional experience of Europe's top restaurants. He keeps a diary exclusively for his meals at Girardet in Crissier. To date, the number of entries is in the forties.

Frédy Girardet, a slim, trim man of about 50 who looks 10 years younger, is a phenomenon. It is remarkable how his restaurant in Crissier, about 30–40 minutes from Lausanne, is unreservedly admired by Europe's leading chefs not normally given to praising their peers.

He lends perfectionism, one of his many gifts, a new meaning. Years ago he mentioned to me his great love for soccer and his life's wish to witness a Cup Final. In due course I surprised him with two tickets. He flew in on the morning of the game — his first visit to London. In the evening over dinner, to which he treated me at the Connaught Hotel, I offered to show him something of London the following morning. To my amazement he refused to stay for a single additional day: to be absent from his restaurant just for pleasure would have been unthinkable, even on his very first visit to London.

His ever-changing combinations of disparate, and sometimes seemingly incompatible, raw materials are dazzling. His endlessly creative ideas click unexpectedly and they are executed with the perfectionist skill of a miniaturist. Spinach, lobster, asparagus, sweetbreads, caviar, sea bass, veal, crayfish and dozens besides — he uses materials like a juggler, who keeps several incongruous objects flying in the air.

One doesn't normally think of the modest cod, underestimated as it is, as a candidate for culinary fireworks. Who would think of upgrading it with a brilliant sauce? Who would, indeed, serve it with a red wine one? And who would dare to couple it with lentils, of all things?! Giradet, of course. Read how he does it and, this time, don't be too diffident to imitate him: the dish is not difficult to prepare.

GIRADET'S COD WITH LENTILS

Serves 4

*4 small cod medallions, about 3 oz
    (75 g) each
1½ oz (40 g) small green lentils
1 sprig thyme
1 bayleaf
Bones of 2 soles
Oil (for frying the sole bones)
¼ onion, diced
¼ carrot, diced
¼ celery stick, diced
½ ripe tomato, chopped
2 teaspoons mixed ground spices*

*(½ teaspoon curry powder, ½
    teaspoon mixed spices, 1
    teaspoon grated nutmeg)
7 fl oz (200 ml) red wine
1 large potato
1 small onion, chopped
3 oz (75 g) clarified butter (see
    page 112)
2 oz (50 g) butter
Salt and freshly ground black
    pepper
Flour*

Soak the lentils in warm water for 2 hours. Cook them with the thyme and bayleaf until they are just tender (approximately 40 minutes), then drain.

Chop the sole bones into pieces and sauté them slightly in the oil. Add the diced vegetables (onion, carrot and celery) and leave to sweat. Then add the chopped tomato, and leave the mixture to evaporate a little. Add half of the mixed spices and allow to cook slightly before adding the red wine. Stir well together, then add 7 fl oz (200 ml) water, bring to the boil and leave to simmer for 20 minutes, skimming from time to time. Strain into another saucepan through a conical sieve and continue to reduce the liquid, skimming occasionally, until it is reduced to ¼ pint (150 ml). Strain it through a muslin cloth.

Peel the potato, cut it into the thinnest possible slices on the mandolin. Wash them in running water to remove the starch, then dry them in a tea or paper towel. Lightly fry the potato in 2 oz (50 g) of the clarified butter until it is cooked and golden but not entirely crisp.

Cook the chopped onion in 1 oz (25 g) butter, until transparent, then add the lentils and warm them until the butter has emulsified and held the lentils together. For the sauce, reheat the reduced stock and whisk in the remaining 1 oz (25 g) butter and correct the seasoning.

Lightly flour the pieces of cod and season them with salt, pepper and the rest of the mixed spice, then cook them in the remaining 1 oz (25 g) clarified butter allowing $2^1/2$ minutes for each side.

Put the lentils, as a base, on a warm plate. Place the pieces of cod on top, so that you can just see the lentils and heap a few potato slices on top of the individual pieces of cod. Pour the sauce around and serve immediately.

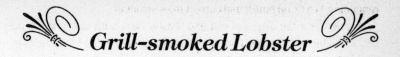

Grill-smoked Lobster

We finally caught sight of the oasis and drove through the gates of heaven, or rather the gates of Les Prés d'Eugénie. A hot day's long, gruelling drive through Central and South-western France had only been relieved by the culinary fantasies with which my driving companions and I were whetting our appetites, lobbing imaginary and tantalising morsels to each other. They were my old friends, the American political journalist, Johnny Apple, whose gastronomic knowledge is unmatched, and his wife. The three-star haven expecting us belonged to Michel Guérard, unquestionably one of France's three or four greatest chefs.

Oasis? A paradise! The air-conditioned rooms are the very lap of luxury, a gorgeous garden surrounds a swimming pool in which we swam a few lengths, readying ourselves mentally as well as physically for a slim but very tall glass of crémant Champagne. Michel Guérard, who knew us well and had received us warmly, suddenly appeared again, apologising for not being able to discuss our imminent feast personally as he was in the middle of preparing dinner for the President of France and his party. In due course the maître d'hôtel asked, '*avec les compliments de Monsieur Guérard*', would we be happy to order exactly the same dinner he was preparing for the President and the same wines? An offer you couldn't refuse.

Unforgettable is certainly the word for what followed. And the paraphernalia reflected the reason why the French still regard the skill, diplomacy and non-servile deference of this level of service as part of a profession well worth pursuing. Eventually Michel, in the relaxed mood that follows success, explained at length that the lobster dish, for a version of which he has recently sent me the recipe (overleaf), had actually been 'cooked' in the smoke of the large fireplace in the dining room.

Some things are worth living for...

GRILL-SMOKED LOBSTER

Serves 2

2 live lobsters, about 1¼lb
(550–600g) each
Vegetable stock
1oz (25g) butter
Sprigs of chervil

Butter and herb sauce
Juice of 1 lemon
4oz (100g) butter, diced
2–3 tablespoons finely chopped
tarragon, chervil, chives and
parsley
Salt and pepper

Kill the lobsters by plunging them into boiling water for 2 minutes. Take them out of the water, remove the claws and cook them in a good vegetable stock for 4 minutes.

Cut the lobsters in two along the length of the body with a pair of scissors, being careful not to damage the meat in the tail. Remove the sack from the head. Take the meat from the shells and set aside. Salt and pepper the shells and place them on a lightly smoking wood barbecue.

While the shells are on the grill, cut the lobster meat and remove the meat from the claws. Put the lobster meat into the shells. Melt the butter and brush it over the lobster meat. Cover, so that the smoke of the grill penetrates the lobster.

Meanwhile, make a butter and herb sauce: heat the lemon juice with 1½ tablespoons of water until it comes to the boil. Remove from the heat and add the diced butter, whisking constantly. Return to the heat and continue to whisk until the sauce is emulsified. Whisk in the chopped herbs and season to taste with salt and freshly ground black pepper.

When the lobsters are hot and smoked, place on a serving dish, spoon over the sauce and sprinkle with sprigs of chervil.

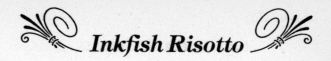

Inkfish Risotto

The original fame of Harry's Bar in Venice was based on Hemingway's regular custom. Today, behind a counter, closely lined from end to end with elbows lifted only to reach for a refill, the barman still mixes the best Martinis — you know, the one with the vermouth bottle being *shown* to the gin without adulterating it.

There is another generation of elbows lining the counter now and the reputation has for a long time been based firmly on the cooking. You visit it for that reason, but you can't help being instantly captured by the excitement in the air, the enthusiastic buzz of conversation, the sun-burnt, sophisticated women at tables packed so closely you can hardly get to yours — if you have the influence to be seated on the ground floor, that is.

Food on the Veneto is no great shakes and in Venice itself you need to be told of good addresses; the Italian Michelin Guide is not as good as the French. However, there is always Harry's Bar — if you can get in. Arrigo (hence Harry) Cipriani still owns it, though he sold the hotel bearing his name years ago. So devoted is he to cuisine that in 1984 he also opened Harry's Dolce at the far end of the Guidecca, away from the tourists, for young Venetians who flock to it for its interesting, inexpensive fare of hors d'oeuvre-type dishes and scrumptious desserts.

As for other good addresses in Venice, I turn to a guide — a human one. He is called Gianni, the incomparable concierge at the Cipriani Hotel. 'Where, again, is that Titian with the kneeling young girl looking at you?' you ask. He will tell you from memory, warning you when the Frari church is closed and possibly drawing your attention to another Titian he finds even more stunning. Luckily, he adores food. 'Mr Ronay', he would say as he has welcomed me enthusiastically, 'this year it's the tiny Da Ivo — *wonderful* pasta! Closed today, though; shall I book at Al Conte Pescaor? It's a little trattoria and you will love the grilled *triglie* (red mullet). And I do.

INKFISH RISOTTO

Serves 6

For the squid

1 lb (450g) small squid
4 fl oz (100 ml) olive oil
1 stick celery, finely chopped
1/2 clove garlic, chopped
1/2 medium onion, finely chopped
1/2 pint (300 ml) dry white wine
6 tablespoons finely chopped mixed
  fresh herbs (including basil and
  parsley)
2 large ripe tomatoes, peeled,
  seeded and diced
Salt and freshly ground black
  pepper

For the risotto

4 pints (2.3 l) chicken stock or
  canned chicken broth
1 small onion, minced
1 tablespoon olive oil
1 lb (450g) long-grain rice
6 tablespoons unsalted butter,
  softened
2 1/2 oz (65g) freshly grated
  Parmesan cheese
Salt and freshly ground black
  pepper

For the squid: Soak the whole uncleaned squid in cold water for 20 minutes. Holding their body sac firmly, pull off the tentacles. Remove the pulp and plastic-like blade from inside the sac if they don't come away with the tentacles. Remove the outer membrane of the sac, wash and set aside. Cut off the tentacles just above the eyes, remove the thin beak-like structure from the base. Remove the ink sac from behind the pulpy matter inside the head, discard the rest of the head.

Chop the body sac and tentacles into 1/2" strips, heat the oil in a large frying pan, add the celery, garlic and onion and cook for 5 minutes until golden. Add the wine and herbs and cook for another 3 minutes. Add the squid and cook gently for 45 minutes, stirring occasionally. Force the ink sac through a fine sieve into the pan and add the diced tomatoes. Season with salt and pepper and continue to cook gently until the squid is tender (about 30 minutes).

For the risotto: Bring the stock to a gentle simmer over medium heat. In a large heavy-bottomed saucepan, cook the minced onion in the olive oil until transparent, add the rice and increase the heat while stirring. Add half the hot stock and bring to the boil. Simmer for 5 minutes while stirring, then add the squid preparation detailed above. Keep a few tablespoons of the stock for the finish and add the rest of the stock gradually, allowing it to absorb before adding more. The rice should be tender though 'al dente'.

Remove from the heat, mix in the Parmesan cheese and softened butter. Add the few tablespoons of stock you have reserved while stirring vigorously, giving it a creamy texture. Season to taste and serve immediately.

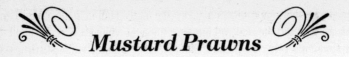

Mustard Prawns

One of the most beautiful modern structures on earth, the Seagram building in New York, houses one of the most attractive and impressive restaurants in the world. The Four Seasons. You ascend a very wide staircase covered with deep-pile carpet and find yourself at the reception desk feeling you have arrived in another sense, too. *Tout New York* is there: the world of Hollywood headed by Elizabeth Taylor, the empires of publishing led by Michael Korda of Simon and Schuster, and Madison Avenue represented by several advertising potentates.

At the end of your ego trip on the staircase, you come face to face with one of the proprietors, Paul Kovi or Tom Margittai, usually standing behind a tall maître d's desk. The quintessence of urbanity and self-assured sophistication, they tell your table number to one of the innumerable headwaiters: you have been imperceptibly assessed. Confess to it or not, there is a shade of embarrassment at having been assigned a table in the far corner; and there is no denying the satisfaction at finding yourself next to the heart of the establishment, a surprising large pool with a fountain, under a five-storey ceiling and surrounded by gigantic windows. You are overawed by the proportions, yet the architect's genius imparts a feeling of comfort.

A suitably splendiferous menu, in size as well as choice, is executed by a Swiss chef; an endless wine list reflecting California's treasures as well as Paul Kovi's unmatched expertise and wine-buying skills; service is far removed from the customary offensive familiarity of American waiters.

The difference between the foregoing and a PR handout is that this one is true. As for the cuisine, see for yourself — one of their memorable dishes, Mustard Prawns, will not disappoint you.

MUSTARD PRAWNS

Serves 4

Italian (Cremonese) mustard fruit is available in tins or jars in
delicatessens, usually sold under the Motta label.

20 large, Dublin Bay prawns
1 pint (600 ml) vegetable stock
For the stuffing
½ x 14 oz (400 g) jar of Italian
  (Cremonese) mustard fruit and
  its liquid
For the batter
4 oz (100 g) plain flour
1 tablespoon olive oil
½ teaspoon baking powder
6 oz (175 g) water
1 egg yolk
Salt
Flour for dipping

For the sauce
3 tablespoons of the same mustard
  fruit
½ oz (15 g) butter
½ oz (15 g) flour
¾ pint (450 ml) fish stock
2 small, level teaspoons mustard
  powder
Salt and pepper
To garnish
Deep-fried parsley
Oil for deep-frying

Poach the prawns in vegetable stock until they turn pink, then drain
(alternatively you can buy them freshly cooked at the fishmonger). Shell
and de-vein.

Mince the mustard fruit with its liquid, but reserve 3 tablespoons for the
sauce. Slit the prawns halfway through and stuff with the minced mustard
fruit. Pack fairly firmly so that the stuffing stays in the prawns.

Make a thick batter with the flour, oil, baking powder, water, egg yolk
and salt.

To prepare the sauce: Melt the butter in a saucepan, add the flour and stir
continuously over a low heat until it forms a roux. Gradually add ½ pint
(300 ml) of the fish stock and simmer the sauce over a low heat for 10
minutes, until it looses its glutinous taste. If the sauce becomes too thick,
add additional stock as required; the finished sauce should be just thick

enough to coat the back of a spoon. Add the remaining mustard fruit and mustard powder and season to taste with salt and freshly ground black pepper.

Roll the prawns lightly in flour, dip into the batter and deep fry in oil until brown (4–6 minutes), then drain. Deep fry the parsley after making sure it is dry (this will spit — so beware).

Serve immediately with the parsley and the sauce served separately.

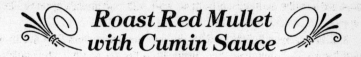

Roast Red Mullet with Cumin Sauce

I once had a dream about my magnificent yacht (it *was* a dream), anchored at Alassio. The steward brought my double cappuccino with an ethereal croissant. I meditated about the turn the conversation might take with my guests over next day's lunch. I planned to find out from Carême, Talleyrand's chef, about his employer's favourite dishes, and hoped that Alexandre Dumas Père (it was going to be a mixed bag) would convince me about his combination of turtle soup and tomato purée that I could never appreciate. The head of the Queen's household should be a most interesting source on the cellars of Buckingham Palace, surely the most breathtaking of all: pre-phylloxera clarets, not to speak of the Tokay Essence from the 1870s that Emperor Franz Joseph must certainly have sent to Queen Victoria.

Then I sent for my chef, Pierre Koffmann, to discuss next day's menu — there is nothing I enjoy more. He suggested we start with a ragoût of oysters, which I love: so we agreed. Then our opinions divided: I said we should follow it with sweetbread ravioli, but he preferred roast red mullet with a cumin sauce. A lighter dish for a July day, his choice prevailed. We both tossed various ideas in the air for the main course: a pity we couldn't very well have yet another fish course because Koffmann's pressed lobster with orange and basil is heavenly, so we toyed with the idea of fillet of lamb cooked in the bag, pigeon with a sweet-and-sour sauce, even beef because of the splendid Italian cèpes with which Koffmann garnishes it. In the end I couldn't resist, yet again, his much imitated and unsurpassed knuckle of pork stuffed with sweetbreads. No discussion was necessary about raspberry soufflé.

Disappointed as I was, when I woke up, that I couldn't meet my dream-guests, I consoled myself that all the dishes Koffmann and I had discussed, and many more besides, he does actually cook at his restaurant, La Tante Claire in Chelsea, London's best. Here is an opportunity to try at least one of the dishes (overleaf). It is not difficult to make and it tastes like a dream.

ROAST RED MULLET WITH CUMIN SAUCE

Serves 4

4 red mullet
2 oz (50g) shallots, cut into chunks
2 oz (50g) leeks, cut into chunks
1/4 pint (150ml) white wine
2–3 pinches salt
2 teaspoons cumin seeds

1/2 pint (300ml) double cream
4 mullet livers (from the cleaned
    fish)
Salt and pepper
1 tablespoon olive oil

Clean and de-bone the red mullet retaining the livers and bones. Cut off the heads and tails. Make a stock: put the bones, heads and tails in a saucepan and add the shallots, leeks, wine and salt. Cover with about 2 pints (1.1 litres) cold water, bring to the boil and skim. Cover and simmer for 20 minutes, then strain, reserving the fish stock.

Boil 3/4 pint (450ml) of the stock with the cumin seeds in it until it is reduced to a syrupy consistency. Add the cream and the mullet livers and boil for 15 seconds. Liquidise the sauce, then pass through a sieve. Add seasoning to taste. Keep warm.

Place the cleaned mullet on oiled foil, skin uppermost. Season with salt and brush the skin with a touch of oil. Put the fish on a baking tray in a pre-heated oven. 220°C (425°F) gas mark 7 for about 4 minutes, or until the flesh flakes slightly when pressed with a finger.

To serve, place the fish on a serving dish and pour the sauce around.

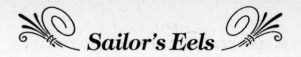

Sailor's Eels

Matelote d'Anguille at Egon Ronay's
Marquee Restaurant, 1953. Chef de Cuisine: Jean Gardes

There is nothing more exciting than opening a restaurant. The creative planning, the outlet it gives to imagination and other talents make the worries, uncertainties, risks and sleepless nights much more exciting than eventual success.

So it was with my last small restaurant, the Marquee in Knightsbridge in 1952. New ideas came up every day. Chef Jean Gardes was as enthusiastic as I, so we led the London scene with *matelote d'anguilles* (recipe overleaf), *chaud-froid de volaille, omelette gratinée*, to mention but a few examples. After a few months, I insisted that the time had come to make *quenelles* of pike, the real thing, of course, not the anaemic version made in a mixer. You couldn't find a genuine one in London. The chef asked for a real, very large mortar, the sort they use in France. Our advertisement in *Paris Soir* was successful and when the mortar, carved from a large, solid rock, arrived at Victoria Station, four porters had to carry it to the van. I suggested to the chef that, to save his precious time, he instruct our young English apprentice how to wield the vast pestle. It was strung up vertically and had to be brought down with considerable force continuously for half an hour to pound the mixture into a homogeneous blend no mixer can achieve. It was heavy work that called for a bit of exhortation. On my way down to the kitchen I quickly turned back, not wanting to spoil the effect of the incentive my full-blooded, Southern French chef offered to our exceptionally shy, English apprentice of 17. He couldn't see me, but I overheard him shouting: 'You 'ave to pound it, you 'ave to pound it and if you can maneege to brrreck the rrrockk, you can sleep with the boss's wife!'

SAILOR'S EELS

Serves 6–8

3 eels of about 1″ diameter (peeled and heads removed)
1 medium onion
3 large shallots
2 cloves garlic
6 oz (175 g) butter
1 level teaspoon finely chopped thyme
2 bayleaves
2 level teaspoons finely chopped parsley

2 tablespoons flour
1½ bottles red wine
1 lb (450 g) button onions
1 level teaspoon salt
1 pinch sugar
½ lb (225 g) rashers smoked bacon
1 lb (450 g) button mushrooms
3 fl oz (85 ml) olive oil
Croûtons
Salt and pepper

Cut the eels into 2½″ pieces and reserve the tails. Finely chop the onion and shallots. Crush the garlic.

Place 2 oz (50 g) butter in a saucepan and sauté the onion and shallots until they start browning slightly. Add the crushed garlic, thyme, bayleaves, parsley and keep stirring. When you can smell garlic, add the flour and keep stirring for 10 seconds. Add 1½ bottles red wine, turn down the heat and keep simmering for about 1 hour.

Meanwhile clean the button onions. Place 3–5 tablespoons water, 2 oz (50 g) butter, the salt and sugar in a frying pan. Add the onions and sauté, stirring occasionally until they start to glaze, i.e. until they are almost cooked.

Cut the bacon into small pieces (i.e. very roughly chop the rashers) and, together with the button mushrooms, fry them in 2 oz (50 g) butter in a frying pan.

Place the eel pieces into a large saucepan with the olive oil, season with salt and freshly ground pepper, and sauté, while stirring occasionally, until they acquire a light-brown colour. Remove the eels and drain on paper towels. Now add all the other ingredients you have cooked, together with the drained pieces of eel, in the large saucepan, adjust seasoning and cook for 10–15 minutes. Serve on a large oval or round dish with a border of croûtons; or serve in a casserole and offer croûtons separately.

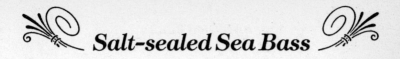

Salt-sealed Sea Bass

My companions, three French gentlemen in their late seventies, occupied perhaps the highest positions in the gastronomic world: the late proprietor of Chez Maxim's; the late Vincent Bourrel, president of l'Académie des Gastronomes; and Georges Prade, the editor of *La Lettre Confidentielle*, a gastronomic newsletter. No wonder that our tour of outstanding French restaurants stands out from my gastronomic wanderings over the years.

Maxim's was a name to conjure with: Vincent Bourrel commanded enormous, nationwide respect and Georges Prade was — and is — beloved by all French restaurateurs. 'Red carpet' would be an understatement: the superstars of the three-star world received us at the door. Like so many princes with their entourage in tow, somewhat deferentially but with great panache, they welcomed the potentates from Paris. Asking for our initial wishes was not in the scheme of things: a prestigious magnum of Dom Pérignon or perhaps Taittinger's Comtes de Champagne was waiting, iced, for the distinguished palates.

There was no question of 'taking our orders'. Serious consultations took place, with the three-star patrons holding forth like eminent professors before complicated surgery, describing preparations in a language as erudite as you would find only in institutions of learning, declaimed in a style worthy of the maîtres at the Court de Cassassion. The results were the most *raffiné* sequences of dishes imaginable, food beyond praise. And the wines! Dazzling experiences of a lifetime, *avec les compliments du patron*.

The only restaurant of our tour with just two stars was Marc Meneau's l'Espérance in Saint-Père-sous-Vézelay, which has long since gained its third star. Here is Meneau's recipe for the uncomplicated dish of sea bass that I recall well after many years.

SALT-SEALED SEA BASS

Serves 4–6

It is the sea water contained in the sea salt that steams the fish. This way of cooking conserves all the flavour.

1 sea bass of about 3¼ lb (1.4 kg)
6½ lb (3 kg) coarse sea salt,
   preferably unrefined
2 oz (50 g) carrots, diced
2 oz (50 g) celery, diced
1 shallot, chopped

1 oz (25 g) butter
½ pint (300 ml) fish stock
½ teaspoon aniseed
½ pint (300 ml) double cream
Salt and pepper
Juice of ½ lemon

Clean the sea bass and remove the fins, but not the scales.

In a cast-iron or porcelain dish big enough to take the fish, place a layer of salt at least ½″ deep. Place the fish on top and cover it with the rest of the salt so that it is closed in its own 'igloo'. Cook in a pre-heated oven 220°C (425°F) or gas mark 7 for 30 minutes.

Meanwhile, sweat the diced carrots, celery and shallot in the butter, without letting them colour. Add the fish stock, aniseed and double cream and bring to the boil. Leave to reduce until the sauce covers the back of a spoon. Add the lemon juice. Season with salt and pepper, as required. When ready to use, pass through a sieve and transfer to a sauce boat.

When the sea bass is cooked, remove it from the oven and leave it to rest at room temperature for 10–15 minutes.

To serve, break the igloo and carefully remove the sea bass. Remove the skin and fillet the fish. Serve with the sauce.

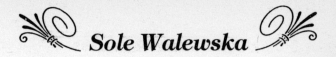

Sole Walewska

Since the new wave of cooking has taken hold, you often don't know what to expect when you read the menu. You are exposed to the experiments of cooks who — with exceedingly few exceptions — overreach themselves. As Len Deighton says in his book, *ABC of French Food*, I like experimenting, but not to be experimented upon. Nowadays, restaurants shun traditional names as if they were afraid of being out of date.

Take those wonderful sole dishes. There was anticipation in names: the flavour of mushrooms in Sole Bonne Femme, crayfish in Nantua, crushed tomatoes of Dugléré, Parmesan in Mornay, cheese and shellfish in my favourite, Walewska (recipe overleaf), are well-high forgotten tastes. Nostalgic memory is all that remains.

With them, coincidentally, the ethos and classic tradition of grand restaurants, too, have almost disappeared. The '96 Piccadilly', of which I was a very young general manager in the 1950s, was one. Elevated to fame through a visit by the then Princess Elizabeth, it was a large establishment of many elegant dining rooms. I would receive *tout Londres* in its lounge and instantly decide whom to seat at which table — an important judgement only to those who did not matter. This was called the art of 'dressing the room', ensuring that easily recognisable VIPs sat where they could be seen instantly from the entrance, flanked by tables with attractive women whoever they may be — a bone of contention with important but older and less attractive women. How absurd it now seems!

The enormous waiting staff was a business within the business. Their greatest concern was for the tronc — the pool of tips — of which the tax people knew nothing. But they knew their business and served, carved, even finished some dishes in full view, like stylish butlers. Their pride in the task and their skill have also gone the way of Sole Walewska.

SOLE WALEWSKA

Serves 4

Mornay sauce

1 oz (25 g) butter
1 oz (25 g) flour
1 pint (600 ml) milk
*1 oz (25 g) Parmesan cheese, freshly
   grated*
1 oz (25 g) Gruyère cheese, grated
2 egg yolks
2 teaspoons water
*4 fl oz (100 ml) double cream,
   whipped*

Main ingredients

8 fillets of Dover sole
Salt
1 oz (25 g) butter
Lemon juice
Fish stock
*4 shelled lobster claws or 8 Dublin
   Bay prawns, cut into ¹/₂" (1 cm)
   pieces*
3 oz (75 g) mushrooms, sliced
*2 oz (50 g) fresh Parmesan cheese,
   freshly grated*
2 oz (50 g) Gruyère cheese

For the sauce: Melt the butter in a saucepan, add the flour and stir to form a roux. Gradually add the milk, stirring constantly until the sauce has thickened. Let the sauce simmer for 20 minutes. Add in the mixed grated cheese and remove from the heat. In a separate pan, combine the egg yolks with the water and set over a low heat, whisking constantly until light and frothy. Do not allow to boil. (This is best done in a bain marie to reduce the risk of curdling.) Fold the egg mixture and then the whipped cream into the Mornay sauce. Keep warm in a bain marie.

Place the sole fillets in a lightly greased dish and season with salt. Add a knob of butter, a dash of lemon juice and just enough fish stock to cover the fish. Cover with wetted greaseproof paper or foil. Cook in a pre-heated oven 220°C (425°F) or gas mark 7 for 7–10 minutes. When they are cooked, remove the fillets on to a clean cloth or paper towel and allow to drain. Place the lobster (or prawn) pieces in the fish stock to warm them through.

To assemble: Divide the sole fillets into four portions and place into four individual oven-proof serving dishes, each with some of the mushrooms —

the dishes must be suitable for placing under a hot grill. Top each dish with a quarter of the lobster (or prawns), cover with the sauce and sprinkle over the mixed grated cheese. Place the dishes under a hot grill until the cheese has melted and becomes crispy. Serve immediately. (Alternatively, the whole preparation can be served on one large oval dish.)

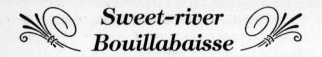

Sweet-river Bouillabaisse

The star role this dish plays in the gastronomy of the Danube Basin is comparable with that of seafood bouillabaisse in French Mediterranean cuisine. The majestic, lazy, grey Danube, river of waltzes and falsely claimed to be blue, has come to symbolise *gemütlich* living. So mild an image sits uneasily alongside the self-assertive personality of this dish. The character of sweet-river bouillabaisse is more akin to another important river bordering on the Danube basin, the Tisza. Fast and unruly, wild in places, it has rich folkloric connections with the fierce and proud race, originally hailing from trans-Ural Mongolia, that used to populate the region, and still does to some extent. That's why old recipes romantically suggest that you *have* to take the water straight from the Tisza and, above all, that the carp *must* be fished from that river. Gastronomically, it makes sense because such carp is leaner.

That brings me to my reluctance to suggest carp, which is usually fat in this country and, God forbid, might even come from a fish farm, its fat reflecting a lazy lifestyle, its flavour echoing mud. The way round it is to try to avoid the older, bigger fish. And you will strengthen the flavour of the dish considerably by adding to its base (the court bouillon) small pieces of some other available fish, such as weaver, grey mullet, herring or cod, though by borrowing from the sea you will obviously be cheating. Still, if nowhere else, at least in culinary matters the end justifies the means.

Don't even think of drinking water with or after it. It may be a soup, but it is related to stews. Remember the Latin saying: *Maledictus piscis in tertium acqua* (cursed is the fish in its third water), i.e. having lived in the first and having been cooked in the second, it must not be cursed by yet another, similar immersion. Given the sturdy character of the dish, it calls for a dryish white wine that will stand up to it without suppressing it. I would quite favour a sauvignon, if its provenance was not Californian since that one would be overbearing. A sauvignon from the Loire would be ideal.

SWEET-RIVER BOUILLABAISSE

Serves 6

Before buying the fish read the remarks about it on the opposite page.

2–3 small-to-medium carp (not big and old ones)

$1/4$–$1/2$lb (100–225g) additional roe (if the carp hasn't enough)

1 medium or 2 smallish onions

$1/2$ very small leek

1 small carrot

14oz (397g) tin of whole tomatoes

5 small-to-medium green peppers (not the large, fleshy ones)

$1/4$ pint (150ml) glass dry white wine

Salt

1 level tablespoon paprika (it must be the 'sweet noble' kind; others will be much too hot

Ask the fishmonger to gut the carp, remove the fish scales and remove the flesh from the spine carefully to free it at least of the large bones. Also ask for the skin to be removed, though not if the carp is small, otherwise the meat might fall to pieces. But you must keep the bones, fins, skin and, if it has been cut off, the head.

Prepare the base, i.e. a court bouillon. *This can be done a day in advance* and kept in the refrigerator. Peel and slice the onion into rings. Discard the uppermost, dark end of the leek leaves. Roughly chop the leek, carrot and the drained tomatoes. Remove the cores of the green peppers, rinse to get rid of the white pips and cut into rings $1/4$" thick. Place all of this, together with the fish trimmings (head, bones, fins, tail, skin), the wine and $1/2$ teaspoon salt in $3 1/2$ pints (2 l) boiling water and cook, at medium heat, for $1 1/2$ hours. Strain by passing it through a conical strainer. Put the debris remaining at the bottom of the strainer in a blender and turn it into a smooth purée. Add this pulp back into the strained liquid, to fortify and thicken it a little, add the paprika and bring it to the boil.

Cut the carp flesh and roe into 2" thick pieces and gently simmer in the soup for 7–8 minutes. Bring it, preferably in a large, rustic casserole or a soup tureen, to the table. First dish out the fish pieces on to large soup plates, then ladle the liquid over them.

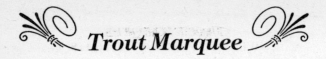

Trout Marquee

at Egon Ronay's Marquee Restaurant, 1953
Chef de Cuisine: Jean Gardes

Usually the preparation of trout does not call for much inspiration. That is perhaps why trout dishes are so dull in restaurants. They print *truite meunière* and the menu acquires a French air. They offer *truite aux amandes*, and skill will — wrongly — be suspected behind this unappealing, basic dish. However, 'blue trout' is anything but dull. The trout is cooked alive, I fear, and thus turns blue. Now *there* is a trout dish! The taste and texture is so delicate that it should be accompanied by nothing but melted butter and a few very small new potatoes without parsley. (Quite delicious with a hock, somewhat drier than the normal run of Rhine wines.) But I must confess that gutting and cooking a live trout takes greater fortitude than most of us possess.

So in the dull days of trout it was something of a revelation when Jean Gardes from the South of France, whom I had engaged as chef de cuisine for my restaurant, first put his recipe to use. We went on featuring it from time to time as *Truite Marquee*. In those embryonic days of gastronomy, the dish drew many clients from the French Embassy. *'C'est remarkable'*, was — and still is — high praise to hear.

The other triumph with fish was *bouillabaisse*. Jean Gardes rightly protested, when I pressed him, that it wouldn't be the same without *rascasse*, a fish unknown to these shores. Anyhow, we had a go and set up a communication system. Fishermen in Cornwall notified our fishmongers in Billingsgate who then telephoned us that, thanks to the weather, they now had all the necessary types and sizes of fish and shellfish. Next day was *bouillabaisse* day at the Marquee. Chef Gardes prepared it freshly (apart from the base) for two people on whom, in those early days, I had to bring all my persuasive powers to bear. To help matters, I translated it on our menu as 'Mediterranean fish hot-pot' — not a bad explanation even today.

TROUT MARQUEE

Serves 6

6 trout (with head on, but gutted)
1 medium onion
2oz (50g) butter for frying onion
6oz (175g) unsalted butter for stuffing, softened
4 eggs, beaten
1 large or 3 small shallots, finely chopped
2 leaves fresh, or 1 teaspoon dried sage

2 leaves fresh, or 1 teaspoon dried thyme
1 tablespoon finely chopped parsley
1 tablespoon grated Parmesan cheese
3 tablespoons fine, white breadcrumbs
1 level teaspoon salt
¼ teaspoon ground pepper
1 glass dry white wine

Wash the trout. Remove the backbones: on both sides of the backbone make an incision at the back of the head near to the bone with a very sharp, small knife and continue down to the tail. This will enable you to remove the spine.

Peel and slice the onion into rings and fry in butter in a frying pan until they just start to colour. Add the removed backbones and keep stirring until the bones become a little soft. Now add 1 pint (600 ml) water and cook gently for 20 minutes. Strain and reserve this fish stock.

Place into a bowl the softened butter, the beaten eggs, chopped shallot, sage, thyme, parsley, grated cheese, breadcrumbs, salt and pepper. Mix with a wooden spoon until it reaches thick mayonnaise consistency. Adjust the seasoning.

Butter two baking dishes and place the boned trout into them, slightly pressed down and flattened so that their backs are wide open. fill these cavities with the stuffing.

Pre-heat the oven to 250°C (475°F) or gas mark 9. Pour the wine and the fish stock around the stuffed trout. When the stuffing starts to colour, cover the trout lightly with foil and place the baking dishes in the top-most part of the oven for 6–7 minutes to make it a little crispy. Then turn down the oven to 200°C (400°F) or gas mark 6 and place them on the middle shelf of the oven for a further 8–9 minutes. Serve immediately.

Meat

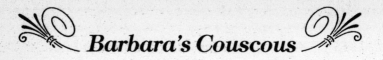

Barbara's Couscous

It may not be the classic recipe, but since my wife adapted it to her own taste after our holiday in Tunisia, adding even non-Tunisian spices, I love it.

It was in Hammamet that we first had couscous and fell for it instantly. Whenever we could, we ordered it. The young maître d'hôtel, admirably trained by a good Tunisian hotel school, was amused by our addiction, and during a chat offered to ask his mother to prepare the real thing for us one day. An opportunity not to be missed. He would take us in his car to his village 30 to 40 minutes away.

We racked our brains as to the gift it would be appropriate to take the lady. Hotel school, car, smooth manners — I put two and two together and decided on French perfume. We couldn't find any in Hammamet, so the gift would have to be sent after the exciting visit.

On arrival, we were faced with the simplest, humblest peasant abode, though endlessly fascinating, with oil and grain storage jars dating back to goodness knows when. The lady turned out to be a nice, extremely simple peasant woman, and the whole family so abjectly poor that they cooked squatting on the kitchen floor because they couldn't afford a cooker, let alone furniture. French perfume — my foot! We ate with our hands, sitting on the floor, the women — though reasonably educated (one a teacher) — standing around in a respectfully distant circle, except for my wife. The couscous was truly memorable and so was the whole experience.

Next day, at my insistence, the young maître d'hôtel shyly agreed to inquire what his mother, who seemed to have stepped straight out of the Bible, would like. We duly sent her a pressure cooker!

BARBARA'S COUSCOUS

Serves 6

This dish is best cooked in a special pot called 'couscoussière'. It can also be made in a large saucepan to which you attach a steamer.

3 oz (75 g) chick peas
3 lb (1.3 kg) lean fillet of lamb
2 medium onions
4 tablespoons olive oil
³/₄ lb (350 g) carrots
2 turnips
2 medium cloves garlic
¹/₂ teaspoon ground cumin
¹/₂ teaspoon ground ginger
¹/₂ teaspoon ground coriander
1 teaspoon turmeric or ¹/₂ teaspoon saffron

Salt and pepper
2 chicken stock cubes
1 lb (450 g) couscous
3 oz (75 g) butter, softened
3 courgettes
¹/₂ lb (225 g) French beans
3 large tomatoes, peeled
3 oz (75 g) raisins
4 tablespoons finely chopped parsley
1 tablespoon harissa
1¹/₂ tablespoons tomato purée

Soak the chick peas in water overnight and boil for 1¹/₂ hours the following day.

Cut the meat into approximately 2″ cubes, peel and coarsely chop the onions. Fry the lamb and onion gently in a pan with 2 tablespoons olive oil. Remove from the heat.

Clean the carrots and turnips and cut into ¹/₄″ slices. Finely chop the garlic. Add these ingredients, along with the chick peas, all the ground spices, 1 teaspoon salt and a little pepper to the pan. Pour in just enough water mixed with the stock cubes to cover the contents. Bring to the boil, lower the heat and simmer, covered, for 1 hour.

Meanwhile wash the couscous and drain well in a sieve. Place in a large bowl and break up any lumps with your fingers. Transfer the couscous to the top part of the covered couscoussière (or to a covered steamer) and place over the bottom part in which the meat and vegetables are simmering. Leave until the steam has penetrated the couscous, causing it to swell slightly.

Remove the steamer and pour the couscous into a large bowl. Mix in the softened butter, 2 tablespoons olive oil, 1 teaspoon salt and ½ pint (300 ml) warm water. Once again, break up any lumps with your fingers. Return this to the steamer and place over the simmering pan to re-heat once more — by now the couscous should be light and fluffy. Remove, cover and leave on one side.

Wash and cut the courgettes into ¼″ slices, trim the beans, chop the tomatoes, and when the meat and vegetables have simmered for 1 hour, add them to the pan with the raisins and parsley. Cover and simmer for a further ½ hour. Towards the end of this cooking time place the couscous (which is in the steamer) over the pan again and re-heat. Before serving, mix the harissa with the tomato purée and a little juice from the pan. As it is too hot for some people, serve separately.

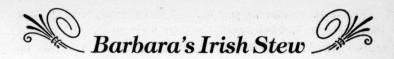

Barbara's Irish Stew

It is said to be simple — and it is. But as with all 'simple' dishes, if you are not careful about the seemingly finicky and mundane details, the result will be poor.

For Irish stew, the selection of meat is most important. Reflect on the time of the year: spring and early summer, irrespective of whether it's warm, is not the time to consider making it. Spring or summer lamb, tender and delicious as it is for other preparations, does not have enough of the essential flavour, not yet having developed its fat. After having used my wife's recipe on the following page, you will appreciate this point: on the morning after cooking, copious fat will have gathered and congealed on top of your pot, ready to be discarded, having infused the whole with the vital flavour it carries. Young lamb would have no such yield and the stew would be essentially without much interest.

It has to be *scrag* of lamb, that is to say the bony bits and pieces of the neck, but ask the butcher to proceed a little further down towards the spine, too, and include *some cutlets from the neck end*, i.e. not those further down from the saddle because they are too meaty. The proof of this dish will be in the succulence of the bony bits.

Another point is that you need an unusually large casserole or pot. Try to avoid making it in two vessels (perhaps borrow a large one from the restaurant you visit regularly?) because — for some reason unknown to me — the larger the quantity, the better the flavours will blend. The vessel should also be respectable and attractive enough to be brought to the table — dishing it out in front of your guests wins them over instantly. The first few soup plates, which must be large, should be filled together, enabling you to vary with meat the helpings of potatoes from the top and to fish out some vegetables.

As you take the lid off, the guaranteed cries of Oh! and Ah! will be a thrilling reward.

BARBARA'S IRISH STEW

Serves 4–6
Make the Irish stew the day before serving it.

6 lb (2.7 kg) neck of lamb (usually the butcher cuts it into chops, cutlets and similar pieces if explained that it is for Irish stew)
2 lb (900 g) large potatoes
3 large onions

4 large carrots
2 sticks celery
2 medium cloves garlic, chopped
Salt and pepper
Chicken stock (instead you can use 1 cube)

Peel the potatoes and onions. Clean the carrots and celery. Cut the potatoes, onions, carrots and celery into ¼″ slices. Divide all the ingredients, including the meat, into two equal portions.

Using the first portion, place a layer of onions followed by the meat, potatoes, carrots, celery and garlic in a heavy-duty casserole. Salt and pepper this layer.

Using the second half of the ingredients, repeat the previous process.

Pour onto all this enough chicken stock to barely cover the contents of the casserole. Bring to the boil on top of the stove. Cover and let it simmer for about 1½ hours or until the meat is just tender. Leave the casserole in a cool place overnight.

Next day, before warming up, remove the layer of white fat which will have gathered on the surface. Heat the stew slowly to simmering point.

Bring to the table and serve in very large, deep soup bowls.

Barbara's Lamb Casserole

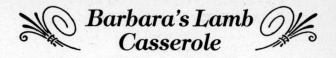

Soon after I married Barbara in 1967, she started experimenting with increasingly demanding recipes. Relishing challenges, within a few weeks she graduated to dishes which, somewhat to my consternation, took several days to prepare. One needed 36 hours marinating, the recipe stipulating that the meat had to be turned every 12 hours.

I was fast asleep at 2 a.m. in our large double bed placed tightly in the corner to make the bedroom more spacious. The shock was quite terrifying when Barbara leaped out of bed, stepping on me and over me (the only way she could get out), clearly in a tremendous hurry and under evident stress. Though unavoidably and suddenly wide awake, I still couldn't believe what I heard: 'I forgot to turn the meat'.

Actually, the impetus of her cooking ambitions came before we got married — well only just. We had been going out for some months, but by no means did I take her agreement for granted when I finally made up my mind to ask her to marry me. It called for cunning. Put her in a romantic mood. Tickets to a good and cheerful play and a call to the maître d'hôtel of our haunt in Kensington, surprising him with my unusual request for a secluded balcony table (it had a pink table lamp). I also ordered a bottle of Dom Pérignon on the table. You can't blame a fellow for trying to create a receptive mood.

Elated after an enchanting play, a quick drive to the restaurant, a glass or two of Champagne, I judged the romantic mood had become irresistible and asked the $64,000 question. Barbara clutched her breast in horror and exclaimed: 'I can't cook!'

The lamb casserole is from her post-marinade period and reflects her great culinary talents.

BARBARA'S LAMB CASSEROLE

Serves 4–6

3 lb (1.3 kg) leg of lamb (net weight after boning)
1½ lb (675 g) tomatoes
Flour for coating meat
Salt and pepper
3 oz (75 g) cooking fat
1 teaspoon sugar
2–3 cloves garlic, finely sliced
1 pint (600 ml) meat stock (or 1½ beef cubes)

2 bayleaves
1 pinch thyme
1 lb (450 g) small new potatoes
½ lb (225 g) carrots
½ lb (225 g) turnips
1 lb (450 g) shallots
¼ lb (100 g) French beans
¼ lb (100 g) green peas

Trim the fat from the meat and cut into cubes approximately 2″ square. Place the tomatoes in a large bowl, pour boiling water over them and leave for 10–15 seconds to loosen the skin. Drain and peel the tomatoes and cut into medium-thick slices. Tip a little flour into a flat dish, season with salt and pepper, and coat the meat with it.

Pre-heat the oven to 175°C (350°F) or gas mark 4. On top of the stove, melt the cooking fat in a large, flame-proof casserole. Add the lamb, about a third at a time, and fry quickly until slightly brown. Remove on to a dish. When the last third is almost brown, sprinkle with sugar, continue frying and stir to avoid sticking, until browned. Remove from the heat.

Return the lamb to the casserole, add the tomatoes, garlic, stock, bayleaves, thyme, ½ teaspoon salt and a little pepper. Re-heat to simmering point on top of the stove. Cover and place in the centre of the oven. Cook for 1½ hours. During this time, scrub the potatoes and carrots, peel the turnips and shallots. Cut the carrots and turnips into chunks. Partly cook the potatoes, carrots and turnips in salted water, drain and leave.

Remove the casserole from the oven and add the partly cooked vegetables and shallots. Cover and return to the oven. Cook for a further 15 minutes.

Meanwhile cook the beans and peas in a saucepan until almost ready. Drain. Remove the casserole from the oven, add the beans and peas, discard the bayleaves. Return to the oven for 10 minutes before serving.

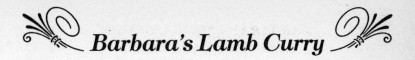

Barbara's Lamb Curry

Until the 1950s you could count on one hand the number of Indian restaurants in London. The best known was Veeraswamy's, overlooking Regent Street, with bamboo furniture imported from India; large palm trees; turbaned butlers; an 80-year-old, dignified major-domo-cum-headwaiter, resplendent in his traditional garb, commanding yet deferential; and a few beautiful girls helping their male masters of ceremony. It has changed considerably since. The atmosphere used to be subdued, and, strangely enough, its memory helped me to appreciate 'Jewel in the Crown' 30 years later.

In those days I knew nothing of oriental cooking, so the major-domo's advice was welcome. Tempted as I was by inviting names such as mysterious vindaloo and exciting chilli peppers, I was guided by him to milder waters. He told me a story about the king of Denmark, exiled in London during the war, who, it was known, used to encourage a macho image to the point of letting his muscular torso be photographed stripped to the waist. On his visit to Veeraswamy's, our major-domo tried to warn him off vindaloo, the hottest of all curries. It was in character that the king ordered it extra hot, and even the old Indian, who must have seen a fakir or two walking on fire or lying on a bed of nails, was amazed that his majestic customer managed to keep a stiff upper lip — or perhaps I should say a stiff upper palate.

Barbara makes a quite delicious curry that will not cause you to wince, though it is self-assertive enough. She quite rightly stipulates that you absolutely must mix your own spices. Using curry powder is like using powdered tea.

BARBARA'S LAMB CURRY

Serves 4–6

2½lb (1.1 kg) lean fillet of lamb
½lb (225g) onions
4 large tomatoes
5–6 medium cloves garlic
4oz (100g) ghee (clarified butter) or
   any animal or vegetable fat
1½" to 2" piece fresh root ginger,
   peeled and crushed
1 level teaspoon haldi (turmeric)
2 level teaspoons dhania (coriander
   powder)

1 level teaspoon jeera (cumin
   powder)
1 level teaspoon garam masala
¾ level teaspoon chilli powder (for
   a mild curry)
1½ level teaspoons hot paprika
1 level teaspoon salt
2 tablespoons yoghurt
6 tablespoons chopped mint for
   garnish (optional)

Cut the meat into approximately 1" square cubes. Peel and slice the onions. Place the tomatoes in a bowl, pour boiling water over them and allow 10–15 seconds to loosen the skin. Drain and peel, cut the flesh into slices. Finely chop the garlic.

In a large saucepan, melt the ghee and add the onions. Fry gently until a golden colour. Mix in the garlic and all the spices. Fry gently for 5 minutes, stirring to prevent sticking. (It may be necessary to add 1 or 2 teaspoons hot water to the pan.)

Raise the heat, add the meat and brown quickly on all sides. Lower the heat and add tomatoes and yoghurt. Cover and cook gently, stirring frequently for 1 hour, by which time the meat should be tender.

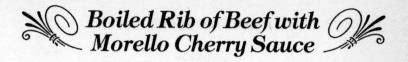 Boiled Rib of Beef with Morello Cherry Sauce

In Vienna, before the first world war, there was a renowned restaurant with a long menu that contained nothing but boiled beef of the highest imaginable quality. It made English boiled silverside look a poor relative. The enormously knowledgeable clientèle was loyal not only to the establishment, but also to its favourite cuts.

There was topside, puritanical perhaps, but, because of its marvellous quality, as tender as butter, melting in the mouth. The lively morello cherry sauce (on the following page) went well with it. The cheapest but still excellent cut was shin of beef, succulent and flavoursome: its ideal complement was horseradish sauce, not the degenerate, creamy, bottled kind, but made on the day with vinegar and sugar. However, purists asked for simple, horseradish, grated, of course, with no addition of any kind. I love it with the spicier variety of frankfurters, but if you try it, do not let it slip too far back on your tongue towards the nasal ducts as it will twist your nose and make you cry. Good for colds, village folk used to say.

Apparently, friendly arguments about cuts of beef were commonplace in Vienna. I would have sided with the rib-of-beef faction, because of the superb tenderness of this cut and the fat flanking it. A simple tomato sauce with it is a solid marriage made in heaven, but it can form an extremely pleasurable liaison with the said morello cherry sauce.

Never forget that fat in meat is the vehicle of flavour. It is depressing that food terrorists and diet demagogues should succeed in preventing us from getting the best. In my father's day, his chefs used to specify 'sugar-factory beet. After processing beet for sugar, they fed it to cattle, a second business for the sugar factories from where Europe's best beef used to come. Marbled texture? The meat used to be almost white with it!

Of what will they deprive us next?!

BOILED RIB OF BEEF WITH MORELLO CHERRY SAUCE

Serves 6

For the beef

6 lb (2.7 kg) rib of well marbled beef
   (not boned and not rolled up,
   only the back bone eased off for
   simpler carving)
1 small marrow bone (with the
   marrow)
1/2 lb (225 g) shin of beef
1/2 lb (225 g) carrots
1/2 lb (225 g) parsnips
1/2 lb (225 g) celeriac
1 small bunch parsley
1 small bunch chives
4–5 whole black peppercorns
3 level teaspoons salt

For the sauce

1 lb (450 g) stoned, tinned morello
   cherries
2 1/2 oz (65 g) unsalted butter
1 oz (25 g) flour
1/2 pint (300 ml) stock (possibly
   chicken cube)
1/2 teaspoon salt
2 or 3 teaspoons sugar (according to
   taste)
1/4 pint (150 ml) soured cream

Clean and cut the vegetables into large cubes. Place all the ingredients listed under 'beef' into cold water and bring to the boil. When it reaches boiling point, remove the scum from the top. Keep cooking until the meat is tender (about 1 1/2 hours, depending on the quality).

For the sauce, drain the morello cherries thoroughly then sauté them in butter for 3–4 minutes. Sprinkle with the flour and keep sautéing for another 2–3 minutes until slightly browned. Add enough stock to achieve a fairly thick sauce consistency, then add the salt and sugar, and finally the soured cream.

Carve the meat in fairly thin slices and discard the vegetables. Serve freshly cooked vegetables if you wish. Serve the sauce in a sauceboat.

The Cassoulet of Languedoc

We went on an abbreviated tour following the trail of medieval pilgrims who walked all through France, weaving their arduous way from cathedral to cathedral until they reached the one on the other side of the Pyrénées at Santiago de Compostela. 'We' means Johnny Apple, his wife and me.

Johnny, one of the foremost political journalists of the United States and an equally eminent gastronome, travels with a veritable library in his car, all manner of books on art and all the existing hotel and restaurant guides to France. It is a sight to behold as he speeds, with the roof open in the blazing sun, holding forth about the Carolingian jewels in Aachen, the best villages for Armagnac, the *tympanum* on the basilica of Conques, the late Allard's guinea fowl in Paris, and occasionally taking a prolonged look, while driving at 70 mph, at the map (or a guidebook, for God's sake!) and worrying me to death.

On our trail of the Romanesque, restaurants had equal importance, and we came across a most memorable cassoulet in a star-less restaurant, the real McCoy from the Languedoc. Its contents being variable, I was eager to find out what had gone into my cassoulet of a lifetime. I wrote for the recipe but the chef-patron, Jean-Claude Rodriguez, had moved to the Château St Martin Trencavell Montredon, Carcassonne (worth noting). I don't know him or his new restaurant, only his cassoulet. My request caused him *émotion et plaisir* and gave him moral support, as he put it in his touching letter, voicing his delight that his dish should be remembered among the architectural marvels of Carcassonne. Michelin has certainly missed out on something here. Let me make sure that you don't.

THE CASSOULET OF LANGUEDOC

Serves 4

7oz (200g) pig's skin
1 pig's trotter
½ knuckle of pork
1 piece of pig's neck
3 bouquets garnis (see method)
1 onion, left whole and studded with cloves
2lb 4oz (1 kg) dried white beans
6oz (175g) onions, finely chopped
3oz (75g) garlic, very finely chopped
4–6 tablespoons goose fat

2 level tablespoons tomato purée
10 cloves
10oz (300g) belly of pork, diced
4 goose gizzards (preserved if possible)
Offal (innards of one goose)
Ground black pepper
1lb (450g) Toulouse or similar sausage
2 goose wings, fresh or preserved

Soak the pig's skin, pig's trotter, knuckle of pork and pig's neck for 3 hours. Add 1 bouquet garni (thyme, bayleaf, parsley, celery), the clove-studded onion and bring to the boil. Remove the scum, then simmer for 1–2 hours and set aside for the next day. Reserve the stock. Soak the dried beans for 12 hours.

On the day of preparation: remove the skin from the trotter and knuckle and cut into small cubes. Discard the neck bone. Press the bouquet garni and onion through a conical sieve to extract the juices and strain them on to the meat cubes. Set aside.

Cook the onions and garlic in 4–5 tablespoons goose fat in a casserole. Add the diced meats from the trotter and knuckle and when they begin to colour, add the tomato purée, a second bouquet garni and 4 cloves in a muslin bag. Set aside.

In a frying pan, brown the diced belly of pork in 1–2 tablespoons goose fat. Drain and transfer to a saucepan with the chopped garlic and onion and the finely chopped gizzards and offal. Wet these with stock from the knuckle of pork and season with pepper. Add the remaining bouquet garni and 6 cloves in a muslin bag. De-glaze the saucepan and skim off any grease. Bring to the boil and cook in the oven at 170°C (325°F) gas mark 3 until the meat is tender. Remove the cloves and squeeze the bouquet garni to extract all the juices. Set aside.

Bring the beans to the boil and simmer until tender, skimming regularly. Drain and combine them with the stock, skin, trotters and the rest of the chopped meats. Mix in the belly of pork and simmer until the white beans jell (they should not be too liquid). Cook the sausages in the oven.

Place the cassoulet in a casserole with the sausages (cut into $3\frac{1}{2}''$ pieces) and the wings of a goose. The skin should be uppermost to become crisp. Cook the cassoulet near the top of the oven for 20–30 minutes. Allow to cool and refrigerate for 48 hours. Re-heat it for 30 minutes before serving. This period of keeping will improve it.

Chinese Long-braised Knuckle of Pork

A dapper, charming Chinese gentleman walked into my restaurant in Knightsbridge 36 years ago to collect his young, pretty English wife of three months who was working for me as a superviser/manageress. That is how I first met Kenneth Lo.

The Lo house was home from home to many oriental and occidental friends, with Ken — as his wife Anne laughingly told me — suddenly having to improvise food often for a dozen or more. That must have been the start of the brilliant culinary career of this gastronome, cook, sportsman, author and raconteur.

The tennis racket of this Cambridge tennis blue (whose father had been ambassador to the Court of St James) is still as important in his life as his wok: a year or two ago, at 71, he came second in the European veteran championship in Monte Carlo. Now he plays only two hours a day!

Soon after our first encounter he taught me how to use chopsticks and we started to make the rounds of outstanding Chinese restaurants for the benefit of readers of my column in the *Daily Telegraph*. One of the first meals off Leicester Square remains the best remembered. Chef Wang, with whom I discussed the heavenly texture of chicken-and-almonds through Ken Lo, did not speak a word of English after 20 years over here. The story was that he had been chef to Wellington Koo, the wartime Chinese ambassador, famous for his table. Later I came across numerous other chefs who made the same claim. But Wang's cooking was genuine.

Some 25 years later, Ken introduced me to the succulence of long-braised knuckle of pork, served to eight Chinese friends, my wife and me at a round table, Chinese-banquet style. Riveting and widely differing delicacies arrive in no particular order, with an oriental disregard for time, as if governed by the chef's mood. Chopsticks reach out from all directions, landing prime bits in your bowl to ensure you don't miss anything. I was well supplied with the scrumptious bits of knuckle, deliciously falling to pieces as they should be.

CHINESE LONG-BRAISED KNUCKLE OF PORK

Serves 4–6

1 knuckle of pork with the skin on,
about 5½lb (2.4kg) before
boning; ask the butcher to bone it
2 tablespoons dark soya sauce
Oil for deep frying
1 pint (600ml) beef stock
2 tablespoons light soya sauce
1 level tablespoon salt

1 level tablespoon sugar
2 tablespoons hoi sin sauce (or
barbecue sauce)
4–5 slices peeled root ginger
2–3 pieces star anise
4–5 tablespoons dry sherry (or red
wine)

Boil a large pan of water. Add the knuckle of pork and boil for 6–7 minutes. Remove and drain. Rub the skin and meat evenly with dark soya sauce. Heat the oil in a wok or deep fryer. When hot, fry the pork for 5–6 minutes and drain.

Preheat the oven to 200°C (400°F) gas mark 6. Place the knuckle of pork in a deep flameproof casserole. Add the stock, light soya sauce, salt, sugar, hoi sin sauce, ginger, star anise and bring to the boil on the stove. Reduce the heat and simmer gently for 15 minutes, turning the knuckle over three times. Close the lid of the casserole firmly and place it in the preheated oven. Cook for 1¼ hours, turning the knuckle over once. Add the sherry (or wine) and continue cooking at 170–180°C (375°F), gas mark 5 for 1 hour, turning over the knuckle gently three times.

Place the knuckle in a large deep serving dish and keep warm. Reduce the sauce in the casserole to half its original volume and pour it over the knuckle just before serving. A knife may be used to carve off the meat into bite-size pieces, each of which must have some skin attached. Usually the meat will be tender enough to remove with a pair of chopsticks and the skin of the pork should be like jelly. It is best with plain rice.

The Original, Authentic Gulyás

Never has a culinary term been so abused and degraded. Small wonder that the name of this soup (for that's exactly what it is, as many will be surprised to read) has acquired an almost pejorative meaning. It isn't all that old — it originated in the last century, its beginnings picturesque, even romantic. Robin Hood-type highwaymen, part of Hungarian folklore, are supposed to have made it first in large, round-bottomed, open cauldrons hung from three converging wooden rods over camp fires. In fact, it still figures as 'cauldron gulyás' on native menus. For some odd reason it has travelled the world since and you meet its wretched derivatives in almost all Western countries, where it is an excuse for inedible, heavily tomatoed, greasy stews, libellously expropriating the name.

Though the recipe opposite is detailed and accurate, certain points are worth stressing. First the paprika you use. It has to be labelled 'sweet noble', ensuring that it isn't hot — this is not a curry! Using tomato purée, whatever any cookery book may say, even semi-official ones sold in Hungary, is no less than outright sacrilege. Don't fall for it.

Then the meat. In this respect, don't take my recipe as gospel. Other cuts of beef (it has to be beef) are acceptable, provided they are not as lean as fillet or silverside. A little rump steak for flavour in the meat selection will not come amiss, though it will not be ideally tender. I understand that before my time most respected cooks would add a little piece of liver and udder, said to improve the flavour further, though that, I would imagine, would be a tall order.

It is possible to serve gulyás as a first course, an apt forerunner to a light, simple fish dish: say roast red mullet or grilled fillets of sole. But it will stand well on its own, followed by one of the last-course pastas (see, for example, pages 198 and 225).

THE ORIGINAL, AUTHENTIC GULYÁS

Serves 5–6

2½lb (1.1 kg) (net weight, i.e. boneless and fatless) beef; about half of it shin of beef, the other half neck
2½lb (1.1 kg) potatoes
Lemon juice
2 green peppers
1 small to medium onion
2 medium cloves garlic

6–7 tablespoons cooking oil (but lard is better)
4 teaspoons 'sweet noble' paprika (this is how it is labelled. It is important as the paprika must not be of the hot variety)
1 glass dry white wine
½ teaspoon caraway seeds
Salt and black pepper

Cut the meat into ¾" cubes. Cut the potatoes into similarly sized cubes and, until used, keep them in a bowl of cold water (with a few drops of lemon juice to prevent them from discolouring). Cut out and discard the stem of the green peppers, cut them lengthwise, each into four parts, peel away the white, inside skin and rinse out the white seeds. Finely chop the garlic and, separately, the onions.

Heat the oil or lard in a comfortable, large saucepan. Add the chopped onions and fry until transparent, but do not brown them, not even lightly. Turn the heat down and add the paprika, mix very swiftly with a wooden spoon (in a matter of 4–5 seconds) and take the saucepan off the heat (otherwise the paprika will darken and the dish will not have an attractive red colour).

Add the meat and stir thoroughly so as to coat the cubes completely with the onion-and-paprika mixture. Return to rather fierce heat and keep stirring for 2–3 minutes so that the meat gets imperceptibly scorched. Add the wine and half a glass of water, the chopped garlic, caraway seeds, salt and black pepper to taste (but go lightly on the pepper). Keep stewing until the meat is almost tender (depending on the meat, this will take about ¾ hour, but you have to test it for tenderness).

While the meat is stewing, partly cook the potatoes for about 7–8 minutes in about 3½ pints of water with half a teaspoon of salt. When the meat is almost cooked and fairly tender, add to it the potatoes and the water in which they were cooked. Bring to the boil and continue cooking for about 8–10 minutes, until the potatoes are done. Adjust the seasoning with salt and not too much pepper.

Serve in large, deep soup plates. A soup spoon should do – the pieces of meat will be small enough not to need a knife and fork.

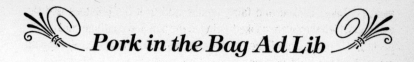

Pork in the Bag Ad Lib

It was going to be a rather special dinner party, four of the guests being my colleagues from the French Académie des Gastronomes. There had been consultations with my butcher a few days in advance and I had given him meticulous specifications for a well-hung, large, marbly fillet of Scottish beef. Being used to my idiosyncrasies, he agreed — I suppose with an inner shrug — to lard the fillet in the prescribed manner with a larding needle, then tie it with equidistant rings of string, but not too firmly, into the right shape for carving. Delivery was promised by 5 p.m., before his closing time. Parisian potatoes I had scooped out in the morning were to accompany the beef, together with grilled mushrooms and Béarnaise sauce.

An old retainer, a friendly pub waitress, came as usual to help with the service and washing up. When I got home, I asked her: 'Is the meat here?' She reassured me. The thunderbolt did not strike until 7 p.m., when I opened the refrigerator intending to pour a little oil and half a glass of good red wine on the beef before spicing it. I was speechless: four fillets of *pork* were staring me in the face! Two orders had been mixed up.

There was no time to fantasise, otherwise I might well have thought of Escoffier in a somewhat similar predicament when Melba, the great prima donna, unexpectedly turned up at the Carlton Hotel after the opera and all he had left in the fridge were peaches, raspberries and ice cream, and of such basic things was peach Melba born on the spur of the moment.

I didn't say a word to anyone (why fish for reproaches?). I sized up the fillets of pork — just right for eight — and checked my stock of tin foil. The only other things I found, apart from the mushrooms, were rashers of bacon and two red peppers. But my improvised dish was a genuine success, as it has often been since. My moment had come: I played Escoffier.

PORK IN THE BAG AD LIB

Serves 6

3 fillets of pork, about 13–14 oz
    (375–400 g) each
½ lb (225 g) button mushrooms (or
    wild mushrooms)
1 red and 1 green pepper

12 rashers smoked bacon
2 medium cloves garlic
1 small bunch chives
3 tablespoons olive oil
Salt and pepper

Cut six sheets of foil, approximately 16″ × 16″, carefully so that there are no holes in them. Cut each fillet of pork in half. Wash and finely slice the mushrooms. Core, wash and rinse the peppers, chop them and mix the green with the red. Cut the rind off the bacon and chop the rashers. Peel and very finely chop the cloves of garlic. Wash and chop the chives (but not too finely). Divide all these ingredients into six equal quantities.

Brush the half-fillets generously with oil (reserve a little for sprinkling) and very slightly season them with salt and freshly ground black pepper. Place each on one sheet of foil. Heap on to them the ingredients in the following order (try to shape them conically so they do not spread more than is unavoidable): chopped mushrooms, chopped peppers, chopped chives, chopped garlic and lastly the chopped bacon. Add another very small quantity of salt and freshly ground pepper. Sprinkle with a tiny quantity of olive oil.

Fashion each lot into well-sealed, foil bags so they do not let out the cooking aromas. There must be no holes in the tinfoil otherwise you loose the essential cooking juices. It is imperative that the bags should be sealed at the ends and as much air as possible left in them so that the ingredients stay loose inside the bags and have enough room for the flavours to fuse.

Pre-heat the oven to 225°C (425°F) or gas mark 7. Place the bags on to roasting tins (you will need at least two) and cook in the oven for 25 minutes. When they are taken out, place each bag on a plate, carefully cut them open and ease away the foil with care so as not to lose any juice. Serve with rizzi-bizzi (rice enough for 6 mixed with a cupful of cooked, green peas).

Potatoed Chops

I prefer to call this dish Potatoed Chops because its French name, *Côtelettes Champvallon*, sounds too high-flown. It is marvellous for winter Sunday lunch in a country cottage with a roaring fire in the next room, where you can sip Armagnac or Port, perhaps after a light dessert such as a chocolate mousse. Almost a one-dish meal, it is not complicated to make.

Try to find a butcher able to supply mutton, but if you are reduced to single lamb cutlets, never use young lamb: they are fatless and lack strong flavour. It is the fat that imparts the vital flavour — hence my recommendation for mutton — and you can always cut off the fat on the plate if you must. Don't cook the onions too much and do use plenty of butter. Clarifying the butter is useful to prevent it from burning and becoming black after two to three minutes even when it has been mixed with some olive oil.

Côtelettes Champvallon was regularly on the menu of my last restaurant (it was frequently served at the boss's table). In restaurants it really comes into its own because quantity enhances the flavour greatly; the potatoes, covering the chops generously and completely, become more thoroughly impregnated with mutton fat, provided you baste assiduously. You will see the difference if you cook it for six or, better still, for eight people. The problem is the cooking vessel, as the chops should really be in one layer at the bottom. If you have to stack them, do change their position during the cooking, but it will need care and skill to avoid breaking up the potatoes in the process.

POTATOED CHOPS

Serves 4

4 chump chops, mutton if available, or 8 fat lamb cutlets (not young)
9–10 medium-to-large potatoes
3 medium onions
³⁄₄ pint (450 ml) chicken stock or chicken stock cubes dissolved in ³⁄₄ pint (450 ml) water

¹⁄₄ glass dry white wine
4 medium cloves garlic, pressed
6 oz (175 g) butter, clarified (see method)
2¹⁄₂ fl oz (70 ml) oil
Salt and pepper

Pre-heat the oven to 230°C (450°F) or gas mark 8. Peel and cut the potatoes and onions into thin rings.

Dissolve the chicken cubes in hot water or use chicken stock. Add the wine and pressed cloves of garlic; mix and keep hot. Clarify the butter by cutting it into small pieces and placing it in a heavy saucepan. Heat gently until melted and foaming, then skim off the surface. Strain the melted butter through a sieve lined with muslin and leave it to settle, then pour off the clear butter leaving the sediment behind. Clarifying the butter like this will stop it from burning later.

Fry the chops, without cutting off the fat, in a mixture of very hot oil and clarified butter for 5 minutes, preferably in a large sauteuse or a very large frying pan, turning them half-way through. Remove the chops. Sauté the onion rings in the same butter and oil until transparent, then remove. Salt and pepper the chops, lay them flat on the bottom of a large casserole, add a quarter of the chicken stock and cook in the pre-heated, hot oven for 10 minutes. Spread the sautéd onion rings on top of the chops, turn down the oven to 200°C (400°F) or gas mark 6, add another quarter of the chicken stock mixture and cook in the oven for a further 10 minutes.

Spread the potato rings over the chops and onions. Add enough of the remainder of the stock, but it must not quite come up to the rim of the chops. Salt and pepper a very little and cook at 200°C (400°F) or gas mark 6 for 35 minutes, provided that all the chops lie flat. If you have been forced to heap chops on to each other, cook for a further 8–10 minutes. Baste every 10–15 minutes.

Serve by placing the chops on plates and evenly spreading onions and potatoes on top. A simple salad, either lettuce or lambs lettuce or radicchio with vinaigrette dressing, is a good accompaniment.

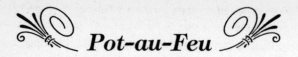

Pot-au-Feu

It hardly needs emphasising that the quality of pot-au-feu almost entirely depends on the quality of meat and the cut you use. It is simple enough to prepare — I always wonder why it is not attempted more often.

There is no definitive recipe. Everyone likes to use ingredients they think contain the secret of success. As for my 'secret', it is to seek out beef which is well hung and, above all, well marbled, that is to say well fattened, not lean, reared by traditional farming methods, for it is the fat that carries the taste — whatever lean-meat-maniacs may say.

Another 'secret' is not to be penny-pinching. If you haven't the heart to buy rib of best Scottish beef, cook something else. But all is wasted if you cut off the little remaining fat when you carve: you kill the succulence of the dish. Equally important, however, is a little shin of beef — it gives the stock its substance and coherence, apart from being a tasty morsel to savour, anyway. As for topside or unsmoked silverside, I use them for the variety of texture they give, but I don't serve too much of it: the glory of the dish, for me, is the rib.

Bone marrow is a great favourite of mine. It always goes down well with our guests. Before the substantial pot-au-feu, that's our first course, particularly when cheese and dessert follow the main course. There are three golden rules about bone marrow: it must be very hot, it should be well salted after having been thickly and loosely spread on the bread, otherwise it is sickly, and the bread, preferably toasted, must be the best. Ideally it should be brown, wholemeal bread and, if not home-made, at least it should *taste* home-made, with the crust on. So there is a fourth 'secret' after all — a traditional bakery.

POT-AU-FEU

Serves at least 6
This dish is best cooked a day in advance.

2 lb (900 g) rib of beef (net weight,
  boned)
½ lb (225 g) shin of beef
1 lb (450 g) unsmoked silverside (or
  topside)
2–3 marrow bones (cut small to fit
  into pot)
4 level teaspoons salt
1½ lb (675 g) carrots
¾ lb (350 g) parsnips
2 oz (50 g) mushrooms
1 small celeriac

1 head of celery
1 small red pepper
½ small or ¼ medium Savoy
  cabbage
6 small turnips
2 medium cloves garlic
2 oz (50 g) tomato purée
Pepper
For the marrow on toast
Bread for toasting
Salt
5–6 teaspoons chopped parsley

Use a very large pot. Place the meat and bones into 7–8 pints (4.2–4.8 l) *cold* water, add 4 teaspoons salt, simmer on very low heat with the lid on for about 50 minutes.

Wash and clean the vegetables and cut up the carrots and parsnips into 1½″ pieces; mushrooms into halves; cleriac into two; discard the leaves and outer sticks of celery and also the top halves of the inner sticks (all of these can be kept for a celery soup, see page 11), use only the bottom halves of the inner sticks cut into 1½″ pieces; core and cut the red pepper into rings; core the cabbage and separate the leaves but leave them whole; peel the turnips but leave them whole if they are young, otherwise halve them; chop the garlic.

Now add all the other ingredients except the mushrooms and red pepper rings. Simmer for 45 minutes with the lid on, then add the mushrooms and red pepper rings and continue simmering for another 45 minutes with the lid on but giving it a gentle stir occasionally. Test the meat: if it still is not tender, carry on simmering until it is.

When the meat is ready, keep the dish in a cool place overnight. Next day, discard the fat congealed on top of the liquid. Bring *slowly* to the boil and remove from the heat. Now remove the marrow bones, put a few ladles of the liquid into a bowl and violently shake the marrow free into the bowl; keep hot in the oven with the door slightly ajar so it does not cook further.

First serve the marrow: spread onto crisp, toasted bread. Salt fairly well — it is too rich without salt — and sprinkle with the chopped parsley. This goes well with a glass of dry, white wine.

Then serve the pot-au-feu: first cut the meat into slices, place some of each cut into deep, large and comfortable soup plates, add some of each vegetable on top of the meat, then cover with the liquid. Some will certainly be left over. It can be kept in the refrigerator and eaten over 2–3 days, or the stock can be used for cooking.

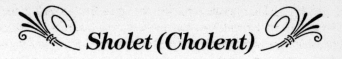

Sholet (Cholent)

A lthough part of the Jewish cuisine (under the name of cholent), this comes from Transylvania where the Jewish minority of 1,000 years' standing had a strong national identity, an important element of which was its cooking. The dish was so popular with non-Jews that it was on the menu of most good restaurants in Budapest and Bucharest. Thursday was its day, as I recall, in one of my family's restaurants where the large quantities prepared were always sold out quickly.

The ingredients were only those approved religiously (kosher) — hence no pork. But there was a most curious sect, a few thousand strong, among the Hungarians in Transylvania, from the 16th to the 19th century, called Sabbatarians, who imitated Jewish religion and adopted some of its rules. They knew better, however, than to adopt those relating to pork, so there was a well-known version of sholet in their region, which used pork instead of beef. It is not a bad idea to have the best of both religious worlds and use beef and pork (boned, smoked knuckle) half and half.

Its long cooking time lent itself to another religious rule: not to cook on the Sabbath. In Jewish communities it was prepared on Friday and eaten on Saturday night — and was very much better for it.

It has some obvious similarity with cassoulet, and since that is one of many dishes made differently in various regions, even households, it wouldn't surprise me if some versions of it came pretty close to sholet. By the way, Mr Heinz could profit greatly by a tip or two from sholet and improve his baked beans formula.

I must warn you that you may not necessarily succeed to perfection the first time because of the imponderables of the quality and the kind of beans you use, the fat content of the beef, and your oven. The second time around you could experiment with pork or maybe change the proportion of beef and goose — favouring goose I would suggest.

SHOLET (CHOLENT)

Serves 6
This should be prepared one day in advance and re-heated.

*1 lb 3 oz (525 g) dried, white butter
   beans*
*1 lb (450 g) salt brisket of beef (with
   the fat on)*
*1 leg of goose (if goose is young, use
   2 legs)*
1 small onion
1½ oz (40 g) lard (or oil)

1 oz (25 g) flour
*2 level teaspoons paprika (only the
   brand marked 'sweet noble' will
   do)*
*2 medium cloves garlic, finely
   chopped*
Salt and pepper

Soak the beans in cold water to cover for 3–4 hours.

Cut the brisket into slices. Bone the leg of goose (do not discard the skin and fat) and cut its meat into large pieces suitable for portioning out when you serve the dish. Peel and finely chop the onion.

Melt the fat in a large saucepan, add the chopped onion and cook until it becomes transparent. Add the flour and stir continuously until light brown. Add the paprika, stir once and immediately remove from the heat. Drain the beans and mix into the contents of the saucepan. Add the beef and goose meat, finely chopped garlic, salt, pepper and enough water for its level to be about 2½" above the contents. Bring to the boil then remove from the heat. Turn the contents into a casserole, cover with a tightly fitting lid and cook in the oven at 160°C (310°F) or gas mark 2–2½ for 6 hours; or leave it cooking in the oven overnight.

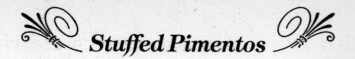

Stuffed Pimentos

Rather flatteringly for pimentos, many nations and regions, all fiercely proud and jealous of their individual cuisines, claim stuffed pimentos as their very own speciality. Once I served it to an Italian who instantly laid claim to it on behalf of his native Naples, particularly as part of my version is tomato sauce. The French maintain that *piments farcis* are part of the *Provençal* heritage. And you can easily pick a pimento argument with people from the Middle East, whether Lebanese, Turkish or Iranian, all of whom make the same claim. If a kind of gastronomic Esperanto existed, this international dish would make an eminently suitable candidate for it, especially since all claimants agree on one ingredient: rice. Everything else, including the meat, differs.

Let them keep their lamb in the Middle East, their mixture of veal plus pork in Germany and Austria, beef and veal in France. To me, such people are culinary deviants. It is pure pork that produces the tastiest result, for the simple reason that the essential black pepper and garlic, which kill veal and vulgarise beef, bring the best out of pork.

As for the pimentos, they are getting more gigantic and, accordingly, firmer, crunchier, more solid and thickly skinned, replacing the better, smaller and a little more flavoured and more subtly textured variety. So rather than falling for the most impressive specimen, opt for the smaller size: it will be much more interesting and have a more prominent flavour.

STUFFED PIMENTOS

Serves 6

6 large (or 12 small) green, red or
    yellow peppers
½ fl oz (15 ml) olive oil
6 oz (175 g) rice
1 lb (450 g) (net weight – without fat)
    lean minced leg of pork
1 egg, beaten

4 small to medium cloves garlic,
    finely chopped
Salt and pepper to taste
2 x 14 oz (397 g) tins whole, peeled
    tomatoes
6 oz (175 g) tin tomato purée
2–3 oz (50–75 g) sugar

Wash the peppers. With a thin, sharp knife, excise the core of each one in a small, neat circle and carefully scrape out the rougher parts of the white lining without piercing the skin. Rinse under a tap to get rid of the pips.

Heat the oil in a saucepan (to prevent the rice from becoming sticky), add the rice and keep stirring for 1 minute. Add about ¾ pint (450 ml) water (exactly double the quantity of rice), bring to the boil, turn the heat down to a minimum and cook the rice for 6–7 minutes. Remove, spread on a plate and leave to cool for 5–6 minutes.

Place the minced pork in a large mixing bowl, add the beaten egg, rice, half of the chopped garlic and season with pepper and salt. Mix thoroughly with a wooden spoon. Stuff the peppers with this mixture, remembering that the stuffing needs to reach their cavities too. The stuffing must not be pressed down too hard, and should leave just a little space between the top of it and the mouth of the peppers, giving enough room for the stuffing to swell during the cooking process.

To prepare the tomato sauce, fish out the whole tomatoes from the tins, place them on a plate, cut them into small pieces and pour them, together with the juice from the tins and the tomato purée, into a saucepan which must be big enough to take, when the time comes, all the peppers in *one* layer. Add the sugar, the rest of the chopped garlic, salt and pepper to taste, bring to the boil, then turn the heat down and gently cook for 10 minutes or so. Adjust the taste with salt and sugar.

Now stand up the stuffed peppers at the bottom of the saucepan in the sauce. Bring to the boil, turn the heat down and gently cook for about 45 minutes. As you will not be able to stir during the cooking, it is preferable to use a thick bottomed saucepan. Serve the peppers each with 3–4 tablespoons of the sauce.

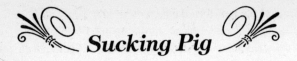

Sucking Pig

At the twelfth stroke of midnight the 750 dignified New Year's Eve customers in my father's immense restaurant went wild. The black ties and elegant, long dresses of 1930s Budapest couldn't keep the lid down. Band full blast, streamer-cobwebbed chandeliers, Champagne glasses clicking, kisses all round, waiters rushing about like Keystone Cops — and suddenly the ear-piercing squeals from a sucking pig cut through the din. It was carried around ritually that night, held down by chefs so everyone could have a tiny snip of its downy hair. This ensured good luck in the new year, backed up by the customary snippet of the patriotically tricoloured ribbon cut by a well-blackened chimney sweep.

The kitchen — resembling, with its herd of sucking pig carcasses and its frantic bustle, something between a veterinary morgue and a railway station — rose to the challenge of 750 simultaneous diners, focusing, by tradition, on the superb, crisp roast. Dishes poured out from behind mountains of plums and peeled apples and a barrage of Champagne bottles, all amassed to enhance the red cabbage: part of the same prescription.

Waiters became diplomats in the vast balconied dining room, serving hind legs to the venerable and privileged, shoulders further down the pecking order. But there was plenty of crisp crackling for everyone, thin and fatless, so swiftly had the heads been cut off the perfectly roasted pigs to prevent sogginess. Gastronomy vied with romantic gipsy violins and madly attractive Hungarian women, at least for a while.

The wonders of those sucking pigs are more easily remembered than described: sweet-tasting, apparently firm meat, yet readily yielding to the fork; thin skin easily and cleanly snapped by the knife. I often wonder what made them so exceptional. The sweetcorn they were fed on? Cooking skill? Stewed apples and plums ripened on the Hungarian plains? Old wine gracing red cabbage? Our youth?

SUCKING PIG

Serves 8–10

A sucking pig of about 14 lb (6.5 kg)
Salt and pepper
¼ pint (150 ml) oil
10 crushed cloves garlic

6 unpeeled cooking apples, cut in
    half
2 bottles of Guinness
1 ripe, reddish Cox apple

For a normal, household oven, cut the sucking pig in half and use two baking trays.

Prise open the pig's mouth and wedge a hard object, such as a stone, between its teeth. If you have forced a wide enough gap, you can replace this with a nice, red, baked apple, or at least a half, before serving. The purpose is to ensure that the heat permeates the head from the inside, the head, and absolutely *all* its parts (not forgetting the ears), being a true delicacy eaten cold the next day. Only the teeth and the bones should be left over.

Wrap the ears tightly in foil and leave this on until the last 25 minutes of roasting to prevent them from being scorched. Salt and pepper the insides generously and brush the skin thoroughly with oil. Line the baking trays with the crushed garlic and apples and turn the pig halves on to them so they rest on their bellies. Salt and pepper the skin moderately. For a 14 lb (6.5 kg) animal, the total baking time is about 2½ to 2¾ hours. Start at 225°C (425°F) or gas mark 7 for 20 minutes. Then cover lightly with foil and continue at 180°C (375°F) or gas mark 5 for 2 hours. Then return to the original, higher temperature for the rest of the time; remove the foil for the last 25 minutes to ensure suitably brown and crisp skin.

Baste every half-hour. During the roasting process, ensure that the meat is not in too much fat, so ladle away some of it. But add a few tablespoons of Guinness after every basting, not on to the skin which it would cool down, but into the bottom of the baking tray.

You must remember to change the top and bottom positions of the trays every 45 minutes or so; and *do keep basting assiduously and liberally every 30 minutes*, doing it extremely fast and closing the oven door instantly both after removing and replacing the trays, so that there is no loss of temperature either in the oven or in the meat.

As soon as the roasting is finished, cut off the head swiftly, so that the steam can escape without rendering the skin flabby; this will also preserve the head in a better condition if you keep and eat it cold the next day.

Serve with red cabbage (see page 178), perhaps also *small* Brussels sprouts, roast potatoes and stewed apples.

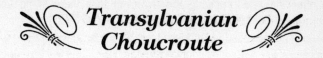

Transylvanian Choucroute

It wasn't the kind of dish you would have in the usual run of restaurants in pre-war Budapest. It needed the right kind of atmosphere, nowhere better than in the small, modest places in Buda on the more sedate, right-hand side of the Danube. 'Let's go to a green restaurant,' one would say in the summer when tables snuggled under huge, ancient trees and one felt securely cradled or, à deux, suitably hidden. They weren't the exact equivalent of bistros or trattorias, except for their intimate size. It was probably out of modesty that none of them was called by the proprietor's name, well known as those gentlemen were (not to mention their wives, whose reputation for homely specialities was widespread). The colourful names, their origins long forgotten, had a faintly romantic undertone: Cuckoo, Marble Bride, Trumpeter, or, more obviously, Ancient Walnut Tree. One of them was simply called — no translation can do it justice — The Little Dirty One, with an endearing twist in my native tongue.

But Transylvanian Choucroute was really more for the winter. In the two rooms that most of such places had, a divided clientèle gathered. The front room, more like a French *zinc*, was for the simpler folk — artisans, coachmen, small shopkeepers and the like — who came for the wonderfully rich and filling soups and, indeed, for Transylvanian Choucroute. Above all, though, they came for the large carafes of inexpensive wine, so young and inferior that it was nicknamed 'knife-opener': its youth gave it a rapid effect that could, on the outskirts of the capital, lead to knifings. The inner room was for regular diners, mostly from the professions, also business people, who all took their food extremely seriously — and looked it. So there was a strict division, symptomatic of the times, but there was no doubt that both camps had a solid common denominator: the excellence of the food, typified by the dish on the following page.

TRANSYLVANIAN CHOUCROUTE

Serves 6–8

This dish is much better cooked 24 hours in advance and heated up.

2 lb (900 g) sauerkraut
2¼ lb (1 kg) lean leg of pork
½ lb (225 g) rice
Chicken stock or cubes
1 medium or 2 small onions
6–7 tablespoons cooking oil (though
    lard is preferable)
1½ level tablespoons paprika (must
    be labelled 'sweet noble'; others
    are too hot for this dish)

1 clove garlic
½ level teaspoon caraway seeds
Salt
½ lb (225 g) smoked, streaky bacon
    cut thick (about 3 times thicker
    than ordinary rashers)
1 lb (450 g) smoked cooking sausage
¾–1 pint (450–600 ml) soured
    cream

Cook ¼ lb (100 g) of the leg of pork in an oven at 225°C (425°F) or gas mark 7 for 50 minutes, cool and mince. Half cook the rice in chicken stock. Cool slightly and mix with the minced pork.

Cut the remainder of the pork into ½″ cubes. Peel and finely chop the onions and cook in oil or fat until they start to colour very slightly. Add the paprika, stir once and remove immediately to prevent colouring. Add the pork and enough water just to cover it. Add the finely chopped garlic, caraway seeds and ½ teaspoon salt. Cook until the meat is fairly tender (about 40–45 minutes), but do not over-cook it as it will be cooked again for the final dish.

Meanwhile prepare the sauerkraut. If it tastes somewhat acidic, rinse well, drain and squeeze out the remaining liquid. Cut the bacon into 1″ strips and the sausage into ¼″ rings.

Grease the inside of a large casserole. Line the bottom with a layer of sauerkraut, then add a layer of rice, followed by a layer each of the cooked pork, bacon strips and sausage rings. Sprinkle liberally with soured cream. Repeat the layers in the same order; again sprinkle with soured cream. Repeat this process, finishing with sauerkraut. (As a few layers are essential, the layers should be fairly thin — depending on the size of your casserole — otherwise you run out of layers.) Pour the sauce in which you have cooked the pork, and the remaining soured cream, on top. Cover and cook in the oven at 200°C (400°F) or gas mark 6 for 35 minutes, then remove the cover and continue cooking for another 10 minutes.

Transylvanian Slushy Cabbage

Most food writers allege that their mother was a good cook, but mine went well beyond that. The third restaurant my father was about to open in Budapest in the 1930s was to specialise in Transylvanian cooking. My mother, not content with her own knowledge, studied old books in libraries about this specialised cuisine, not only discovering scrumptious recipes, but also unearthing endearing names of dishes such as 'Slushy cabbage' or 'Calvinist heaven' (a dessert).

In the large, busy brasserie, pretty waitresses, in very full and short Hungarian peasant skirts and white stockings, rushed about displaying amazing skill at weaving among the tables with their trays bearing foam-headed glass mugs of mouth-watering beer and bulging, steaming, open casseroles. You could catch the tempting whiff of food if you were lucky enough to be sitting downwind. The waitresses and the rich smells disturbed and intrigued the senses of the late teenager I then was. Double-glass screens, each framing a different piece of hand-embroidered folk art, formed a box surrounding very heavy teak tables, uncovered but scrupulously scrubbed, in the centre of fixed wooden benches. What a wonderful atmosphere of conviviality it all created!

But the heart of it all, at the head of numerous cooks, was Chef Papp whom my mother trained in the art of this unusual cookery. In those days chefs weren't a law unto themselves. Even so, he sorely tried her patience, but her irresistible charm and diplomacy, power of persuasion and, above all, her infallible palate, won the day in the end. The place was an overwhelming success from the day it opened.

Transylvania, after France and China, produced one of the world's three greatest cuisines. Peacefully cohabiting Hungarians, Saxons, Jews, Walachians and Armenians were the ingredients of this thousand-year-old, liberal melting pot, which was also an age-old caravan route. A stunningly varied, sumptuous cooking resulted, most herb-conscious and blissfully innocent of dietary reticence, a gastronomic bridge between East and West. Opposite is one of the links in this bridge.

128

TRANSYLVANIAN SLUSHY CABBAGE

Serves 6
This dish is even better if it is prepared the day before.

2 small white cabbages, cored and cut into $1/3$" strips
2 lb (900 g) shoulder of pork
6–8 rashers smoked bacon
1 medium onion, finely chopped
$1/2$ teaspoon black peppercorns
6 juniper berries
12 leaves fresh summer savory (or $1/2$ level tablespoon dried summer savory or tarragon)
10 sprigs fresh dill

2 bayleaves
3 or 4 ripe tomatoes, skinned, seeded and chopped
2 tablespoons rendered lard or butter
$1 1/2$ level tablespoons flour
4 fl oz (100 ml) soured cream
1 egg yolk
1 tablespoon tarragon vinegar
Salt and pepper

Place the cabbage in a saucepan and just cover with lightly salted water. Bring to the boil and cook briefly so that the cabbage is cooked but just firm. Drain, retaining the cooking water.

Simmer the pork in this cabbage water until almost done (about 1 hour), remove and slice, but again keep the cooking liquid.

Line the bottom of a large pot with the bacon. Cook until some fat is rendered, add the chopped onion and keep cooking until the onion becomes glossy. Remove from the heat. Add a 1" layer of cabbage strips, sprinkle with a few peppercorns and juniper berries, then cover with a layer of the sliced pork. Tie the savoury and dill together into a few, small bunches. Add one bunch of the herbs to the pot (or sprinkle generously with the two dried herbs) and $1/2$ a bayleaf.

Place on top another layer of cabbage strips, then peppercorns and juniper berries, then meat, a bunch of herbs and another $1/2$ bayleaf, leaving enough for yet another layer of the same combination. Add the chopped tomatoes. Top all this with your last layer of the same combination of meat, cabbage, peppercorns, juniper berries and herbs.

Pour on the cooking liquid you have set aside. It should cover the last layer completely. Cover and cook on low heat for 1 hour until the meat and cabbage are tender.

Make a roux with the lard (or butter) and flour to a golden brown colour. Beat into the roux, until smooth, the following mixture: the soured cream, egg yolk, vinegar and 4 tablespoons of the liquid from the pot. Pour this mixture into the pot, then slowly simmer until it thickens. Season to taste with salt and pepper.

(The difference of using fresh herbs makes it worth the trouble of finding them. If necessary, spare ribs can be used instead of the shoulder of pork.)

Transylvanian Stuffed Cabbage

Transylvanian cuisine is magical. It is tragic that it should be part of an endangered culture, together with Transylvania's exceptionally beautiful folksongs. Bartók and Kodály went around villages early this century preserving hauntingly sad motifs. They listened to peasant women singing lullabies, singing while doing their washing in the mountain streams, singing to ease every chore of the day, songs on which the two giants eventually based some of their best music (for example Kodály's fabulous 'Peacock Variations'). Improbably, their example was followed in the gastronomic field by one of the two proprietors of the Four Seasons, New York's world-famous restaurant — Paul Kovi, himself a Transylvanian. For 20 years he has spent his holidays travelling from village to village collecting half-forgotten recipes of this extraordinary, scrumptiously flavoured cuisine, rich in herbs and cross-fertilised by five races living in harmony. (His *Transylvanian Cuisine* is published by Crown Publishers, New York.)

The names of dishes themselves were unusual and playfully colourful, for example Wedding Soup, Students' Pie, Tailor's Soup, Highwayman's Meat: pleasing in the native tongue to musical ears.

Stuffed Cabbage, its native name indicating that it comes from Kolozsvár, the old capital of Transylvania, has been preserved with a vengeance: it is on the menu of every restaurant worth its salt in Hungary. Usually it is vulgarised by the meat in the stuffing and by the lard they use. As you can see, even in its classical form it is not to be approached except with something of a trencherman's appetite.

TRANSYLVANIAN STUFFED CABBAGE

Serves 6

1 lb (450 g) leg of pork (net weight
   without fat)
2 lb (900 g) tinned sauerkraut
6 oz (175 g) rice
6–7 tablespoons oil
1 egg, beaten
3 medium cloves garlic
Pepper and salt
1 large cabbage
1 large onion

3 level teaspoons 'sweet noble' (not
   hot) paprika
1/2 glass dry white wine
8 thin rashers smoked, streaky
   bacon
1 1/2 tablespoons flour
1/2 pint (300 ml) soured cream
Optional:
6 slices raw, 1/4" thick smoked loin
   of pork
6 small smoked cooking sausages

If the sauerkraut is too sour, very lightly rinse it in a strainer under cold water, but it mustn't lose acidity altogether.

Heat a teaspoon of the oil in a saucepan, add the rice and keep stirring for 1/2 minute over high heat. Add about 3/4 pint (450 ml) water, turn the heat down to the minimum and part-cook the rice for 6–7 minutes. Strain if there is liquid left. Remove, spread on a plate and leave to cool for 5–6 minutes.

Mince the leg of pork and mix thoroughly with the beaten egg, rice and half of the chopped garlic. Season with pepper and salt.

Separate the leaves of the cabbage without breaking them. Steam or cook them until they get limp and easy to fold. Carefully cut out the thickest part of the stalks only from bottom end of the leaves. Now fold the leaves round lumps of the meat mixture to form parcels 3" long and about 1 3/4" thick and neatly tuck in both ends.

Finely chop the onion and heat in the remaining oil until transparent. Add the paprika, stir very fast for 3–4 seconds only and immediately remove from the heat. Add the sauerkraut and mix well, add the wine and the remainder of the finely chopped garlic. Salt and pepper to taste. Divide the sauerkraut into two lots; spread half at the bottom of a comfortable casserole, place the stuffed cabbage leaves on top, cover with smoked bacon, then cover with the rest of the sauerkraut. Cook gently on the stove for 40–45 minutes.

Remove the stuffed cabbages. Thicken the sauerkraut with a smoothly blended mixture of flour and soured cream. Place the stuffed cabbages on a serving dish, cover with sauerkraut and spread the bacon rashers on top. (Optional: add the cooking sausages to the sauerkraut for the last 10 minutes of cooking, fry the smoked loin of pork and arrange both around the sauerkraut before serving.)

Poultry and Game

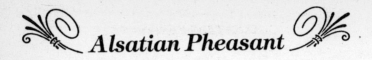

Alsatian Pheasant

Don't even consider pheasant, let alone prepare it, without a larding needle. Do not believe those who try to reassure you that covering the bird with lard or bacon is just as effective. Simply not true. It is just one of the controversies that have been kept on the boil by gastronomes, probably ever since the Argonauts, who are said to have introduced pheasant to Europe as a by-product of their quest for the Golden Fleece. How to hang pheasant and for how long? How to cook it? What is the ideal age for the table and what time of the year to shoot it?

But back to the vital larding needle, a sharp-pointed instrument with which to introduce ⅛″ thick strips of larding fat (with a useful, thin membrane on one side) or the fat cut from streaky green bacon. Do it assiduously, i.e. densely, for it makes the drier birds succulent. As for hanging, this must, of course, be done when the pheasant is still undrawn and unplucked. Nowadays, conscientious game butchers will do it properly (five to six days is my own preference). But you must, I am afraid, smell the inside to judge: if it hardly smells at all, it has been drawn prematurely; if it smells really putrid (if — to call a spade a spade — it stinks), it is too far gone. It is best not to have it too early in the shooting season, because it takes a few weeks for the pheasant to acclimatise itself to the wild and the natural food after its release from the pen where it has been fed. Christmas to January is its high season.

Don't be conventional: roasting is not the only — I dare say, not even the best — way to prepare it. Try, for example, sealing it in a boiling bag or tinfoil, folded so that it is watertight; but first lard it, then stuff it well between the breast meat and the skin with wild — or ordinary — mushrooms, calves liver, smoked, streaky bacon (all finely chopped and bound with some beaten egg), and add a glass of Port or Madeira and four to five nuts of butter before sealing the bag. After some 45 minutes' gentle cooking in a pot on top of the stove, the result will be gorgeous.

ALSATIAN PHEASANT

Serves 4

2 pheasants
2 lb (900 g) tinned sauerkraut
10 rashers smoked, streaky bacon
1/4 lb (100 g) mushrooms
1/2 lb (225 g) chicken liver (or goose
    liver or pâté de foie gras)

1 medium clove garlic
1 egg, beaten
Salt and pepper
4 tablespoons cooking oil
1/2 bottle good quality, dry white
    wine

Give the sauerkraut a rinse in cold water.

Prepare the stuffing: cut the rind off 3 rashers of bacon and finely chop with the mushrooms (after discarding the stalks), the liver and the garlic and mix with half of the beaten egg. Salt and pepper to taste.

Lard the pheasants with a larding needle, using thin strips of bacon from 2 rashers — 2 strips in each side of the breast and 2 in each leg. (If you have no larding needle, cover the pheasants well with smoked bacon rashers.) Carefully separate the skin of the pheasants, only where it meets the tip of the breast bone, and with your fingers ease the skin gently off the meat as far down towards the neck as you can without tearing it. With a coffee spoon, ladle the stuffing through the opening you have cut and ease it forward with the handle of a spoon by pressing towards the neck. Continue on both sides of the breasts so it bulges nicely, all the while watching that the skin does not tear. After having used up all the stuffing, sew up the opening you have cut and any tears you may have inadvertently caused. Salt and pepper generously the insides of the birds and brush all over with oil.

Heat the sauerkraut and keep it hot without actually cooking.

Place the pheasants into a pot with the remainder of the oil and 1/4 bottle white wine. Place the remaining bacon rashers on and around the pheasants, cover and cook gently on the stove for 25 minutes. Now remove 2–3 rashers from around the pheasants, dice and mix them into the heated sauerkraut and ladle this mixture on top of the pheasants. Pour on the remainder of the wine, cover and cook gently for another 20 minutes. Remove the pheasants, carve and serve them garnished with the sauerkraut and bacon and with boiled potatoes.

Barbara's Cucumber-sauced Chicken

I am so sorry for the humble cucumber. It is treated with contempt almost from its birth. Swathed and choked in a plastic, skin-tight stocking, it is left on the shelf in its prime, without as much as the dignity of a date stamp, until it cannot fulfil its destiny properly any more. Regarded as a second-class vegetable, neglected and treated inconsiderately, it is altogether undervalued, its hidden treasures missed. Poor, tragic cucumber.

would think of buying special equipment to give it a better start in life when a knife is all it is supposed to need? Yet, that strangely named kitchen utensil, the mandolin, can set it on the road to better things and — hard to believe — to eventual glory.

Without such help it is reduced to nothing but a shape added to mixed salads just for that, crudely and inconsiderately cut into thick discs, rendering the ridiculously tight salad bowls in restaurants even more difficult to grapple with.

Its delicacy is overlooked. Like water colours, it must never be applied too thickly. Our grandparents knew better. Cut to near-transparency and tenderly nursed between two ever-so-thin slices of excellent, fresh, white bread, with the lightest smear of salted butter, the cucumber was the pride of British teas.

In salads, too, it should be very thin, best achieved with the mandolin. But that's not enough: after slicing, it should first be soaked in generously salted water for eight to twelve hours, then squeezed as dry as possible by hand. Indeed, that's when it graduates to a solo appearance in the wonderful cucumber salad, with its costume jewellery of red and black pepper, and wearing a small, jaunty hat of soured cream.

Then to its apotheosis: this chicken dish of which the sauce, unlikely as it may sound, is infused with a most delicate flavour of cucumber.

BARBARA'S CUCUMBER-SAUCED CHICKEN

Serves 8

2 medium onions
2 large carrots
2 large tomatoes
12oz (350g) butter
¼ teaspoon dried thyme
2 bayleaves
Salt and pepper

2 large cucumbers
16fl oz (450ml) double cream
1 heaped tablespoon 'sweet noble'
    paprika (not the ordinary, hot
    variety)
2 x 3½–4lb (1.6–1.8kg) roasting
    chickens

Cut the onions and carrots into slices. Place the tomatoes in a bowl; pour boiling water over them and allow 10–15 seconds to loosen the skin. Drain and peel. Slice into quarters, remove the seeds and chop the flesh coarsely.

Melt 5oz (150g) butter in a large baking dish or casserole and fry the onions until softened. Add the carrots, tomatoes, thyme, bayleaves, ½ teaspoon salt and a couple of turns from the pepper mill. Leave aside. Peel the cucumbers, slice lengthwise into four parts and remove all the seeds. Slice into segments ¼″ thick.

Bring salted water to boil in a saucepan. Remove from the heat, spoon in the cucumber segments and leave to blanch for about 3 minutes. Drain.

Melt 7oz (200g) butter in a large saucepan and stir in 10fl oz (300ml) double cream. Add the cucumber, a little pepper, ½ teaspoon salt and the paprika. Cover the pan and stew over a gentle heat, stirring occasionally, for about 10 minutes until cooked. Remove from the heat and leave aside.

Gently re-heat the vegetables in the baking dish on top of the stove. Place the chickens on the vegetables and spoon a little of the liquid over each. Put the baking dish in the oven and bake at 220°C (425°F) or gas mark 7 for 1 hour until cooked. Baste frequently.

When the chickens are cooked, remove them from the dish. Either carve or place the chickens on a serving dish and keep warm.

Pour the remaining 6 fl oz (175 ml) cream into the baking dish and heat on top of the stove until bubbling. Remove from the heat and strain the juice into the cucumber and cream mixture. Discard the vegetables. Check the seasoning and adjust if necessary.

Bring to the boil while stirring. Either pour the sauce over the chickens or serve separately in a sauce boat.

Chopped Breast of Goose and Creamed Beans

Apart from being one of the homeliest dishes, this is also useful in another way I shall explain. Normally goose is a festive dish, not something to attempt frequently. It never goes quite as far as in theory. There is hardly anything I adore more than a roast leg of goose, but by the time it is cooked to perfection, the breast dries out a little and I am left with the drier part in deference to my guests.

But if you use the breast for the dish overleaf, you kill two parts of the same bird with one stone. You can, with a very sharp knife, make a clean cut along the breastbone, release the skin and fat, ease them back on both sides with a knife and cut the two breasts off the bone with surgical precision. Then sew the skin together along the breastbone tightly and proceed with roasting. You can keep the breasts in the refrigerator for a day or two (not more) for the goose breast recipe.

The creamed beans are only an example of the way you can prepare other vegetables, too. Lending themselves best to this method are spring greens, Savoy cabbage, fresh peas, medium-large carrots and spinach. The advantage is that they serve as a sauce deliciously permeated with the taste of the vegetables. They lend any number of roast birds, joints and grills a new lease of life.

It is not a fashionable method because of the minute flour and fat content, exaggerated out of all proportion. And I certainly wouldn't argue that young — and I mean *really young* — vegetables, particularly when picked a few hours before cooking, are exquisite when slightly cooked and just turned in butter. But if you think of plainly cooked, anaemic vegetables on a side dish, they are just not in the same league as these creamed ones.

CHOPPED BREAST OF GOOSE AND CREAMED BEANS

Serves 6

Breast of goose

Breast of 1 large goose (or breasts
    of 2 small geese) about 12 oz
    (350g) total
1/4lb (100g) fat leg of pork
1/2 pint (300ml) milk
1 fresh white bread roll, about 2 oz
    (50g)
2 oz (50g) smoked bacon
2 oz (50g) goose fat or lard
2 oz (50g) finely chopped onion
1 medium clove garlic, finely
    chopped

1 pinch dried marjoram
2 tablespoons chopped parsley
Salt and pepper
2 eggs, beaten
1 1/2oz (40g) breadcrumbs

Creamed beans

2 lb (900g) runner beans
Salt
1 1/2oz (40g) butter
1 1/2oz (40g) flour
1/2 pint (300ml) soured cream

Method for breast of goose: Cut the bread into pieces and soak in milk for
1/2 hour. Cut the goose breasts off the bone. Chop, *as finely as you possibly
can*, both the goose meat and pork. Cut the bacon into very small pieces.

Fry the bacon pieces in the fat, together with the onion until the onion is
transparent. Add the garlic, marjoram and parsley, and continue frying for
a minute or so. Cool slightly and add all this to the chopped goose and pork.
Strain the milk from the bread, put the chopped meat and the bread into a
food processor or mixer and process until well mixed. Add most of the
beaten eggs but keep some for brushing the meat before baking. Add the
breadcrumbs and mix thoroughly. Season to taste. Remove from the
processor (or mixer), shape into a loaf, brush with left-over beaten egg,
cover with foil and bake at 200°C (400°F) or gas mark 6 for about 1 hour,
while basting every 15 minutes.

Method for creamed beans: Wash and string the runner beans and cut
into about 1 1/4" lengths. Place into slightly salted boiling water so they are
just covered. Cook on high heat for about 5 minutes or less, depending on how
old they are.

In a separate saucepan, make a light roux: heat the butter, add the flour and stir thoroughly and constantly until the roux just starts colouring, but don't let it brown. Take off the heat, add 2 ladles of the liquid the beans were cooked in and stir vigorously with a whisk or a wooden spoon to get a smooth texture without lumps. Add this to the saucepan containing the beans and their cooking liquid; stir, add the soured cream and bring to the boil. Serve with the chopped goose breast by way of garnish and sauce.

The Classic Paprika Chicken

Finding a *real* paprika chicken is a rare discovery indeed. Chicken Macbeth would be a more apt name for the heavy-handed restaurant versions made, I imagine, by witches rather than chefs. Unscrupulously they add hot red pepper, as if it were a hot curry, and use a boiling fowl, as if prolonged tenderising were a substitute for flavour. They add tomato purée, the nostrum of sloppy chefs, and then administer the *coup de grâce*, an overdose of black pepper, actually a blessing in disguise, as it anaesthetises the palate. A mouthful makes me itch to bring an action under the Trade Descriptions Act, except that we are not quite ready yet for testing gastronomic values in court.

The ideal bird for this dish is free range or, at the very least, not frozen and as fresh as possible. The paprika must be labelled 'sweet noble'. The onions should not be browned, just starting to turn blond. Chicken liver, one for each bird, is a useful addition and real chicken stock is a bonus. If you have forgotten to buy soured cream, cook something else rather than substituting ordinary cream. And if food terrorists have given you inhibitions about melted-down bacon fat or lard, forget the whole thing.

Accompanying paprika chicken with rice or potatoes is like wearing a top hat for tennis. The only conceivable thing is *galuska* ('gawlooshka' is the nearest I can get to the pronunciation), sometimes translated as 'small dumplings', which it is not. Gnocchi, its heavier and stickier third cousin, would be nearer the mark. It is simple to make by lightly mixing ½lb of flour, the yolk of a large egg, half a cup of double cream or soured cream, a cup of water and half a teaspoon of salt, to a reasonably loose consistency; then tearing or cutting small teaspoonsful as you keep dropping them into fiercely boiling water. When they surface, they are ready. Heat a little lard with very little soured cream, roll the *galuska* in it and rush to serve it immediately. Just typing it makes my mouth water.

THE CLASSIC PAPRIKA CHICKEN

Serves 8

*2 chickens, about 3–3½lb
(1.3–1.6kg) each
6–8 small chicken livers
1 large or 2 small onions
1 small green pepper
4oz (100g) lard or, preferably, the
equivalent amount of fat
rendered from green bacon*

*3 heaped teaspoons paprika (must
be labelled 'sweet noble': do not
use any other paprika for this
dish)
About 1 pint (600ml) chicken stock
(if necessary, cubes will do)
1 teaspoon salt
7floz (200ml) soured cream*

Dissect the chicken into legs, thighs, breasts, wings and parsons' noses. Wash the chicken livers and carefully remove any remainder of bile. Finely chop the onion. Remove the stalk from the green pepper, rinse out all the pips and cut it into rings (you will be using half of these for decoration).

Sauté the chopped onion in the fat, in a large saucepan or sauteuse, until golden brown. Add the paprika, stir once and *immediately* remove from the heat otherwise the paprika turns dark. Add all the chicken pieces, put the saucepan back on the heat and keep sautéing while constantly stirring with a wooden spoon until the skin is slightly scorched (about 6–7 minutes). Add stock, barely to cover the chicken, otherwise the sauce will be too liquid, the livers, half the pepper rings and the salt. Simmer until the chicken is tender (about 35–40 minutes, depending on the quality of the chicken). If you see that the sauce will not be enough, add a little more stock as you go on, without making the sauce too liquid.

Remove the chicken pieces and keep warm. Remove 3–4 tablespoons of the sauce and mix thoroughly with the soured cream until smooth. Add back into the sauce and stir. Place the chicken pieces on to a large serving dish and pour the sauce on top. Top it with 2 or 3 (not more) pepper rings by way of decoration. Galuska (see opposite page) is the classic accompaniment.

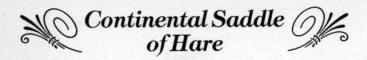

Continental Saddle
of Hare

Nothing can replace hare, particularly saddle of hare, but I have to tell you that its continental sauce, which I like to call game sauce, can be used to fake game dishes. Fake is perhaps too strong a word, and it is certainly worth your while to try a beef dish with the sauce of the hare. You will be surprised how much it imitates a true game dish.

The way to proceed is to boil a small joint of beef (say unsmoked silverside or sirloin) with diced carrots and parsnips, a small piece of celeriac or a stick or two of celery, peppercorns, a bayleaf, some very thinly pared lemon peel, a few juniper berries, three tablespoons brown vermouth, two tablespoons brandy and a glass of red wine. Prepare the game sauce separately, as described in the recipe on the page opposite, but with the addition of some of the cooking juices of the beef. Arrange slices of the boiled beef on a large, oval dish, cover with the game sauce, sprinkle some chopped parsley on it and serve either with boiled, small potatoes or, better still, with some thin tagliatelle and buttered, preferably young, carrots.

As for hare, even though some people might find the test a bit gruesome, I would suggest you make sure that the hare is fairly young. Buy in the fur at a game butcher and, before having it skinned, test it by tearing its ear: if it tears easily, it is young. And you will have the opportunity (another gruesome detail) to ask the butcher for some of its blood, unless — as the recipe suggests — you have ordered it in advance.

In Central Europe it is invariably served with bread dumplings. Putting it briefly: cut three one-day-old, white bread rolls into very small cubes; mix very smooth pastry with two eggs, a nut of butter, 1 lb (450 g) flour and enough water to result in texture neither too hard nor too soft; add the bread roll cubes, shape into dumplings 1½–2″ diameter, cook in fiercely boiling water, then roll in hot butter-and-oil mixed with a tablespoon of soured cream. Mmmmm!

CONTINENTAL SADDLE OF HARE

Serves 4

For the marinade
(24–36 hours in advance)
$^1/_2$ bottle red wine (preferably a
    youngish Rhône)
4 tablespoons brown vermouth
2 tablespoons brandy
$^1/_4$ pint (150 ml) olive oil
1 diced carrot
1 diced parsnip (optional)
1 bayleaf
6 peppercorns
6 juniper berries
2 strips of thinly pared lemon rind
Main ingredients
2 saddles of hare of good size (not
    too young), each cut into 2 pieces
$^1/_4$ pint (150 ml) hare's blood
    (ordered in advance from the
    butcher)

6 rashers smoked, streaky bacon
    (2 for larding, 4 for cooking)
$^1/_2$ medium onion, finely chopped
3 fl oz (85 ml) cooking oil
2–3 medium carrots, diced
1 medium parsnip, diced
2 tablespoons brown sugar
juice of $^1/_2$ lemon
$^1/_4$ bottle dry white wine
6 oz (175 g) prunes, cooked, stoned
    and mashed in a food processor
$^1/_2$ wine glass brown, bitterish
    vermouth (e.g. Punt e Mes)
2 tablespoons brandy
1 teaspoon Dijon mustard
3 tablespoons soured cream
3–4 pinches salt
4–5 turns of the pepper mill

Mix all the marinade ingredients in a large casserole. Clean the thin skin off the saddles carefully with a very sharp, small knife. Place the saddles in the marinade and leave for 24–36 hours.

Remove the saddles from the marinade but keep the liquid. If you wish, lard the meat with very thinly cut strips of streaky bacon, with a larding needle. Dice the remaining four rashers of bacon and fry, together with the finely chopped onion, in 2 tablespoons of oil in a large, comfortable frying pan or sauteuse, for 3–4 minutes over fierce heat. Add the remaining oil, the saddles, diced carrots and parsnips and continue frying, over fierce heat, for another 3–4 minutes. Turn the contents of the frying pan into a large saucepan. Add all the other ingredients listed, except the soured cream. Now add all the marinade.

Cook at medium heat for about 50–55 minutes, or until the meat is tender. Remove the saddles, place on a heated serving dish and keep warm.

Liquidise the whole sauce and pass it — and press it — through a conical strainer into another saucepan. If necessary, adjust the seasoning of the sauce according to taste with salt, pepper, brown sugar and lemon juice. If the sauce is not thick enough (aim at the consistency of a *very* thick soup), thicken it further by adding the debris (puréed in a blender) left at the bottom of the conical strainer. Remove $1\frac{1}{2}$ cups of the sauce, blend with the soured cream by whisking in a bowl and mix into the rest of the sauce.

Pour the finished sauce over the saddles. Serve blackcurrant jelly with it. A good accompaniment is a small helping of pasta, either the wider *papardelle* or narrower *tagliatelle*. An alternative is rice mixed with lightly fried, thinly sliced mushrooms.

Len Deighton's Chicken Tarragon

It was perhaps inevitable that my first meeting with Len Deighton, well over 20 years ago, should take place in a restaurant. The owner of the Trattoria Terrazza in Soho, where we met, was Mario Cassandro (half of Mario and Franco), a close, mutual friend, and I had avidly followed, some years before, Len's cookery strips in the *Observer*.

It seems strange now that the food connection used to be Len's main claim to fame. I regard his subsequent years of multi-million readership, films, TV series, his arrival at the pinnacle of the world of thrillers, merely as an interlude between his years of training in some of France's great restaurants and his new book: *ABC of French Food*. Many people will see this book as an unexpected development, but I prefer to think of it as a U-turn. The world is like the stage: taste it once and you will always hanker after it. Len's nostalgia culminated in the new book, a fascinating, individual, instructive collection of very personal views about innumerable food topics, many of them treated almost lyrically, the subject being very evidently his first love.

Indeed, he keeps something of an adulterous relationship going, having married into the world of spies. He is a constantly practising cook, with a stockpot permanently on the go. His sous-chef (I should say co-chef) is his attractive wife, Ysabele, while his two teenage sons make intelligent and receptive apprentices.

Our many get-togethers over the years have all been convivial, our conversations inevitably drifting back to the subject of food and wine. One important topic is chicken tarragon, for which we share a mutual enthusiasm. Hence his recipe.

Len recollects many variations, among which one is a fricassée with tarragon at La Mère Blanc and another is with chervil, mint, parsley and basil at Troisgros.

His dish, he told me, "does make for a white on white look that some 'creative' chefs might not like, but I usually eat it with eyes closed".

LEN DEIGHTON'S CHICKEN TARRAGON

Serves 4

1 excellent quality chicken, about
   4–5 lb (1.8–2.2 kg)
2 big handfuls fresh tarragon
1 medium onion, chopped
1 medium carrot, chopped
1 slice bacon, chopped

6 fl oz (175 ml) dry white wine
4 fl oz (100 ml) double cream
1 medium clove garlic, finely
   chopped
1 egg yolk

Put the chicken (loosened and with all strings and trussing removed) in a large roasting bag, with a big handful of fresh tarragon inside the bird. In the bag alongside the chicken add the onion, carrot, bacon, wine, cream and garlic. Roast at 200°C (400°F) or gas mark 6 for about 1 hour — an additional 10–15 minutes may be needed for a large chicken.

Strain all juices from the bag, reserve them and put the chicken aside to rest.

Put lots of fresh tarragon leaves (not the stalks) into a blender, chop finely and add to the beaten egg yolk. Slowly add the strained chicken juices to the egg yolk, beating as you do it. This juice should be hot enough to make the yolk thicken the sauce. If it is not, use a double boiler to warm it so the yolk binds to make a thin sauce. Or if there is too much juice, reduce it over high heat before adding to the yolk.

Remove the skin before serving. Decorate with tarragon leaves if you wish. Carve it at the table and serve with plain boiled brown rice, with extra sauce to hand. A good, chilled Beaujolais drinks very well with it.

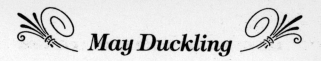

May Duckling

The *Hangli*, a vast garden restaurant in Budapest, was one of my family's establishments before the war. In a way it was a substitute for the private garden many of its regulars would have liked to possess: shaded by ancient trees, relaxing and not a hundred yards from the Danube, on what was called the *Dunakorzo*. This was a fashionable promenade which acquired world renown overnight thanks to the marksmanship of King Edward VIII, then Prince of Wales. From his balcony at the Ritz, overlooking the promenade, he shot out the gas lights of the street lamps at dawn after a night on the town. Far from causing complaint, this excapade actually filled the people of Budapest with pride! The *Hangli* was home from home for a well-heeled clientèle of bankers, stage stars, lawyers, wealthy burghers, doctors, civil servants, aristocrats and nouveaux riches, with a sprinkling of well-born and well-connected layabouts — in other words of fascinating, stimulating reflection of pre-war Budapest.

In May the seasonal dish was May duckling, the first of the season in those pre-battery days, always served with a salad of wafer-thin cucumber slices. What happened to young ducklings? Where have all the poussins gone? May ducklings were just enough for two and came out of the oven with their skin crisp yet succulently lined with the thinnest imaginable layer of fat. Their tender meat had a flavour half-way between chicken and goose, much more marked than that of today's ducks. Does cucumber salad go better with any dish? And what looks prettier than a side plate lined with it and decorated, from rim to rim, with the sign of the cross, vertically with black pepper, horizontally with red? Perhaps it originated in some monastery — monks in that part of the world didn't abstain from the sensuous pleasure of eating.

MAY DUCKLING

Serves 2–3, depending on size

1 duck, the smallest, youngest you can buy, about 4 lb (1.8 kg) if possible
Pepper and salt
1 small clove garlic
1 fl oz (30 ml) cooking oil

For the salad *(soaked a day in advance)*
1 large cucumber
Salt
Paprika ('sweet noble' variety, not hot)
Black pepper
¼ pint (150 ml) soured cream

Method for duck: Remove the trussing string and chop off the feet. Bend the legs firmly away from the breast with your hands to let the hot air circulate efficiently during the roasting. Loosen the bottom cavity so as to be able to spice the duck easily inside. Stand the duck on its neck end, lean it against something to support it and spice the cavity very liberally indeed with pepper and salt. Place a crushed clove of garlic into the cavity. Smear oil all over the skin with a brush. Pre-heat the oven to 225°C (425°F) or gas mark 7. Roast a 4 lb (1.8 kg) duck for 70 minutes, basting it every 20 minutes, twice during the last 20. Every time discard some of the melted fat so that the bird can roast and does not stew in fat. Carve the duck into 6 pieces: 1 breast from each side, each leg cut into 2 pieces at the joint. Carve carefully so as to keep the crisp skin intact.

Method for cucumber salad: Peel the cucumber and slice it as *thinly as you can* either on a slicer (mandolin) or with a thin, very sharp knife. Put 4–5 teaspoons salt and the cucumber slices in a bowl of cold water and *leave overnight in the refrigerator*. Before serving, take as many of the slices as you can manage in the cup of your hands and squeeze as hard as you possibly can several times to get rid of all the water. Carry on until all the cucumber is reasonably dry, but do not dry with a cloth. Arrange in a flat layer on side plates. Sprinkle paprika sparingly but so as to 'draw' a single, continuous, horizontal line from rim to rim of each plate. Then cross this, 'drawing' a vertical line of black pepper by carefully turning and manipulating the pepper mill. Place a blob (about 1 tablespoon) of soured cream in the centre of each cross.

Serve with new potatoes, skinned, turned in butter and sprinkled liberally with chopped parsley.

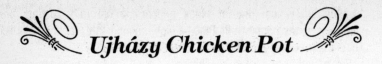

Ujházy Chicken Pot

It is very rare that a chef names a dish after one of his customers because he has inspired it or even chosen the way it is cooked. It can only happen to someone of great fame, such as Alexandre Dumas, who was an inspired amateur cook himself and even wrote about gastronomy. His eponymous consommé is served with a blob of fresh, ripe tomato purée which you are supposed to mix into the consommé just before eating. (Between ourselves, I would have found his dish most forgettable, except that I once complained about it at Maxim's in Paris and they politely shut me up by explaining its sacrosanct credentials.)

Ujházy was a celebrated actor of the National Theatre in Budapest early this century and a considerable gourmet. Not for him the ordinary chicken soup. He knew what he wanted and had the authority and experience (and the chefs of the day had the receptiveness) to prescribe the ingredients. He would not be surprised at having been forgotten as an actor after all this time, but he would be amazed that his name should have been perpetuated by a chicken soup, still a staple of menus in his city.

I have no idea what had motivated him to ask for the addition of spring cabbage leaves or French beans or — a master stroke — the vermicelli that really makes the dish. Shamelessly, I take liberties with the dead man's copyright and slightly adapt my own version, for a very good reason: flavour. Not that his original had been lacking, but boiling fowl of his day were natural birds, their taste not obliterated by chicken factories; they had more fat to which the natural feed pecked from peasant courtyards imparted what I now have surreptitiously replaced. That is why I use smaller birds, not boilers.

UJHÁZY CHICKEN POT

Serves 6–7

1 boiling fowl of about 5–5½ lb
   (2.2–2.4 kg) or 2 chickens of
   about 3–3½ lb (1.3–1.6 kg) each,
   and all their giblets
6 oz (175 g) rib of beef (not too lean)
1 small piece of marrow bone
Salt
½ lb (225 g) carrots
¼ lb (100 g) parsnips
½ of a small or ¼ of a large
   celeriac

1 green pepper
½ Savoy cabbage
¼ lb (100 g) French beans
2–3 oz (50–75 g) mushrooms thinly
   sliced (or dried wild mushrooms)
2–3 fleurons of a cauliflower
1½ teaspoons tomato purée
½ lb (225 g) vermicelli (pasta)
1 small bunch parsley, finely
   chopped

Place the beef and marrow bone into 6–7 pints (3.6–4.2 l) water and add 4
teaspoons salt. Slowly bring to the boil, turn down the heat, cover and
gently cook for about 10 minutes. Add the chicken and the giblets and
continue cooking, very gently at low heat, for another 30 minutes if the
chicken is a boiling fowl, or 15 minutes if you use two smaller chickens.

Meanwhile, clean and cut the carrots and parsnips into 1" long pieces,
or ½" thick rings. Peel and cut the celeriac into two. Wash, core and cut the
green pepper into rings ¼" thick. Wash and core the Savoy cabbage and
separate its leaves. Wash the French beans and cut off their ends.

Now add all the other ingredients, except the vermicelli and parsley.
Bring to the boil, turn it down to very low heat and simmer very gently until
the chicken and the meat are cooked (about 2 hours). Cook the vermicelli in
a separate saucepan (about 7–8 minutes).

Remove the chicken, the giblets and the meat from the saucepan.
Remove the saucepan from the heat. De-grease the soup by syphoning off
the fat and finish the de-greasing by applying paper towels several times,
like blotting paper, to the surface of the soup. Remove all the meat from the
chicken carcass. Cut the chicken meat and the giblets into pieces about

$1\frac{1}{2}''$ long, and the beef into small cubes of about $\frac{1}{2}''$. Take the marrow out of the bone by shaking it free.

Distribute all the meat, giblets, marrow and the vermicelli into the 6 to 7 soup plates, which should preferably be large and deep, and add a little — not too much — of all the other vegetables except the celeriac but including the parsley. Now ladle on the soup and serve.

Sandwich Gâteau

It was going to be the gastronomic tour of a lifetime. My two companions-to-be, the president of l'Académie des Gastronomes and Louis Vaudable, proprietor of Chez Maxim's, arranged it around 3-star restaurants in France. Clearly, red carpets would be rolled out. Planned rendezvous, 12.30 in Paris at Maxim's.

Just a cup of coffee and a single slice of toast at 7.30 a.m. before my flight. Banking on 12 medium Belon oysters and some light fish at Maxim's merely to pacify digestive juices already anticipating the wonders in store at our dinner at Troisgros. But, disaster — flight delayed. Frantic and starving, reach Maxim's at 2.45 p.m., pleading, embarrassed, for sandwiches to take, but lacking the guts, for hours, to unwrap the neat tinfoil in Vaudable's super Bentley driven by his Portuguese chauffeur-cum-valet. Semi-deliriously fantasising about tea parties decades before, with glorious 'sandwich gâteaux'. Suddenly, hunger becomes sidetracked: Bentley breaks down on the way to Troisgros at 5.30. Two hours unsuccessful thumbing for a lift flanked by my two octogenarians. Eventually undergo surrealistic ride in the Bentley on the elevated top of a break-down lorry (a motorised elephant ride hugely entertaining for passing motorists), to arrive at a north Burgundian village garage. Seats are upturned crates in patches of oil-drenched sawdust. Heart-breaking telephone cancellation of Troisgros table. Thirteen hours since my slice of toast!!!

All of us ravenous, myself near fainting. Vaudable: 'The sandwiches!' Valet springs into action, tinfoil is unwrapped, then — *deus ex machina* — garage keeper's wife appears with a bottle of Burgundy. Valet to the fore and, slapping his white handkerchief onto his arm, pulls the cork with his pocket knife-cum-corkscrew. Negotiating the oil slicks, offers a little (*comme il faut*) to his boss. Vaudable, in the surrounding slum, ceremoniously sniffs and tastes. A moment's silence, then: '*Mes compliments, Madame*'.

Finally, a century after my morning coffee, my teeth sink into the most unforgettable sandwich of my life.

SANDWICH GÂTEAU

Serves about 10

1 very light, white loaf, 8–10″ long,
e.g. Sainsbury's 'large white loaf';
best of all a brioche bread from a
good pâtissier

For salmon layer
3 oz (75 g) poached salmon
1 oz (25 g) butter
1 tablespoon finely chopped dill
1 teaspoon freshly pressed lemon
juice
Salt to taste

For egg layer
3 eggs
1 tablespoon soured cream
2½ teaspoons Dijon mustard
½ tablespoon very finely chopped
parsley
Salt and pepper to taste

For smoked mackerel layer
3 oz (75 g) smoked mackerel
¼ oz (20 g) butter
½ teaspoon freshly pressed lemon
juice
2–3 turns of the pepper mill

For liver layer
6 oz (175 g) fine-textured liver pâté,
e.g. Sainsbury's 'pork liver pâté'
2 tablespoons brandy

For decorating
6–7 small red radishes, cut in half
2 tablespoons finely chopped
parsley
½ finely chopped green pepper
2 tablespoons Danish (or real)
caviar
Finely chopped egg whites left over
from egg layer

Cut all the crust off the bread. Slice *horizontally*, with a long, thin knife to obtain five layers, each about ¼″ thick. Prepare the four spreads.

Salmon layer: Mix the ingredients thoroughly in a blender.

Egg layer: Hard-boil and cool the eggs, but use the yolks only and save the whites for decorating the top of the gâteau. Mix with the other ingredients thoroughly in a blender.

Smoked mackerel layer: Bone the fish and mix thoroughly with the rest of the ingredients in a blender.

Liver pâté layer: Mix the ingredients thoroughly in a blender.

Spread the four different layers as if you were preparing a gâteau (but leave about one fifth of each filling for covering the gâteau when it is finished). Lay the fifth slice of bread on top of the prepared layers. Cover all four sides and the top with the spreads you have saved. Decorate the top of the gâteau, and the sides more sparingly, as if you were decorating a normal gâteau. (Do not mix up the fillings — use separately to create a pleasing visual effect.)

Keep in the refrigerator for at least 2–3 hours before serving. It will keep for 2–3 days, but you may have to refresh the decoration.

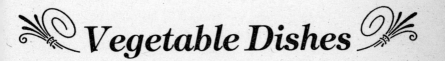

Vegetable Dishes

Aligot

The siege of Budapest was over. Army, police, electricity, transport had all gone West, fleeing the Russians. We emerged from the cellar into the deep-frozen January morning. Twelve members of my family gathered in my flat. The first acceptable food we ate was mashed potatoes with cheese sprinkled on it for nourishment. I remembered it 40 years later when I came across a memorable *aligot* (recipe opposite) in Central France at the marvellous little restaurant of the Hotel Moderne in Espalion.

One of our large family restaurants with some 750 seats had been used by German tanks as a short cut between two streets. There were no windows left, the temperature was minus 20°C, mercifully preventing an epidemic and enabling the population to hack meat off the army's dead horses in front of our ruined restaurant. The streets were empty, all shops were closed. But in one's twenties, life cannot stop. Two of our old headwaiters appeared, and we cleared a small corner of the restaurant, 'requisitioned' a tiny, wood-fired stove from an empty flat, broke up a few restaurant chairs for fuel and started brewing ersatz coffee; the retreating Germans had taken everything else with them. I scrawled 'OPEN' on a piece of large cardboard, and misspelt it in the excitement. Ill-clad cellar dwellers emerged, unbelieving; so did my perennially elegant uncle in brown trilby and with a piece of string tied around the waist of his navy blue cashmere overcoat to make allowances for the circumstances. General consternation: two armed Russian patrols approached, but all they wanted was to *buy* cups of hot coffee! I served them.

Russian patrols were capturing people at random, instantly transporting them to labour in Russia and to oblivion. When I went in search of a loaf of bread for my twelve 'lodgers', I ran into a patrol and was hauled, terrified to death, into the barracks nearby. We were vetted: middle-class background equalled Siberia. A miracle! My guard was the Russian soldier I had served three days before. My desperate sign language conveyed: 'Tovarish ... I serve ... waiter ... work with my hands ...' He remembered, broke into a smile and translated. I was free. And a memorial plaque, still on the building, commemorates the first premises of any kind that opened after the siege.

ALIGOT

Serves 6

This is a simple dish, but not easy to achieve well. Use good boiling
potatoes such as Maris Piper or Cara.

1³⁄₄lb (800g) potatoes, peeled
¹⁄₄–¹⁄₂ pint (150–300ml) milk,
* warmed (see below)*
1 lb (450g) Tomme de Savoie cheese,
* rind removed and coarsely*
* grated*

3oz (75g) butter
Optional: garlic, or lard
Salt and pepper

Place the potatoes in cold salted water, bring to the boil and cook for 20
minutes, or until the potatoes are tender when pierced with a knife. Drain
the potatoes and, with a wide-bottomed, mushroom-shaped pestle, pass
them through a drum-shaped, fine wire-mesh sieve into a saucepan.

Over a low heat, add the warmed milk to the potato and beat the
mixture together to make a firm purée consistency — the exact amount of
milk to be added depends on the type of potato used. Add the cheese and
butter a little at a time so that they melt. You can add a little garlic or
melted lard to add taste. Season with salt and freshly ground black pepper.

Bubble and Squeak De Luxe

While cabbage builds you up medically, it tends to drag you down socially. But I recall one memorable evening when the humble cabbage was elevated far beyond its customary social standing.

The particular variety on the page opposite was perhaps the most homely dish in my native country, a frequent accompaniment of joints and grills. It featured, perhaps somewhat incongruously, on the menu of the Society Restaurant in Jermyn Street (now called Tramp), a beautiful, wood-panelled dining room, sophisticated, elegant and frequented by the cream of society. I was its general manager, my first job in England.

One day in 1948 or 1949 a table was booked for Princess Margaret and her party. I wanted to do my best to 'dress' the room, as they used to say, with suitable young couples preferably in dinner jackets, but I only had 24 hours in which to do it.

A month earlier, an impecunious, 20-year-old emigré friend, who came from a very good family and was studying at Manchester University, had asked for my help and a job. All I could offer him was £5 a week to spend eight hours a day in a tiny basement room cleaning the large number of huge, silver candelabra that were a hallmark of the restaurant. But it was to him that I turned in my predicament on the day of the Princess's visit. Did he have a girlfriend? (A superfluous question to ask a Hungarian.) Did he have a dinner jacket and his girlfriend an evening dress? They did. I gave him the afternoon off to get organised and on the dot of 7.30 my dashing and smart silver cleaner, with a ravishing girl on his arm, was received by my reverent headwaiter who didn't recognise him (Professor Higgins would have been proud), and placed him, as I instructed, next to where the Princess was due to be seated. Next morning at 8 a.m. sharp he was back in his basement chrysalis from where he had emerged for a royal evening.

I remember exactly what the Princess had to eat, her main course accompanied by what I feel should be dubbed Bubble and Squeak de luxe.

BUBBLE AND SQUEAK DE LUXE

Serves 6

2 Savoy cabbages or 5–6 spring
  greens
7 lb (3.2 kg) potatoes
2 medium cloves garlic
Salt

1/4 teaspoon caraway seeds
1 teaspoon white wine vinegar
1 1/2 oz (40 g) butter
1 3/4 oz (45 g) flour
1/4 pint (150 ml) soured cream

Cut away the hardest core of the cabbages (or spring greens), discard the dark outer leaves, wash and cut the remaining leaves into approximately 4"–5" pieces. Peel the potatoes and cut them into about 3/4" pieces. Peel and finely chop the garlic.

Place the potatoes and garlic into about 3/4 pint (450 ml) salted, boiling water and add the caraway seeds and vinegar. After 7–8 minutes' boiling time, add the cabbage (or spring greens), mix and keep boiling for another 3–4 minutes.

Meanwhile, make a roux: melt the butter, add the flour and keep stirring all the time with a wooden spoon until it takes on a light-brown colour. Take off the heat and add a cup of cold water and mix forcefully to prevent lumps forming. Then add a cupful of the cooking juice, again mixing thoroughly until it is entirely smooth. Pour it back into the potatoes and cabbage, mix and keep boiling for 1/2 minute. At the end it should have the consistency of a very thick soup. Before serving, add the soured cream, bring to the boil and serve.

This happily accompanies any roast or grilled meat or fowl.

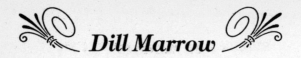

Dill Marrow

You wouldn't believe that marrow could be turned into something to write home about. Let alone rave about.

To call it a side dish would degrade it. It must not be separated from what it accompanies (more about that anon), as it is supposed to be not so much a vegetable, but a sauce containing vegetable. To draw a parallel: when you have fish in a white wine sauce, for example, it is the sauce that should merit attention more than the fish. And so it is with dill marrow.

I am not sure whether the master stroke of blending with it a purée of pickled cucumbers (only those pickled with dill will do) and adding liquid from the cucumber jar to the cooking juices, comes from Victor (ex-Gay Hussar, Soho), a great synthetist of flavours, or whether it has always been part of my original recipe. It was he who reminded me, some time ago, of the magical purée touch.

As with sauces, it is important to serve it with the right kind of meat, although on occasions I have served this dish on its own, after a simple main course, with great success. People are incredulous that it's marrow they are eating. Don't serve it with beef — it doesn't taste the same — or with lamb. It will do with roast birds, but it really comes into its own with veal. Strangely enough, it also goes with a roast loaf of minced meat, particularly of goose breast (see page 141), which is how Victor used to put it on his menu.

Does it seem strange to go on about marrow, that orphan of vegetables? I can only say that the proof of the marrow is in the eating.

DILL MARROW

Serves 6–8

6–7 small-to-medium vegetable
  marrows
Salt
3 large pickled cucumbers (must be
  pickled in dill; best from a Dutch,
  Polish or Hungarian jar)
4 medium onions
4 large tablespoons goose fat or lard
  or butter and olive oil mixture

½ pint (300 ml) liquid from pickled
  cucumber jars
5 heaped tablespoons finely
  chopped fresh dill
½ pint (300 ml) soured cream
Optional:
1½–2 level tablespoons flour

Peel the marrows and cut them in half. Scoop out the interiors with a tablespoon and keep for later. Slice and cut the flesh into thick spaghetti shape: you can do this either by using the corrugated blade of a mandolin slicer, or with a large, sharp kitchen knife. Now sprinkle lightly with salt and leave for 2–3 hours. Then squeeze them dry.

Purée the pickled cucumbers finely in a blender.

Peel the onions, cut them into halves and thinly slice them. Melt the fat in a saucepan, add the onions and cook until transparent. Now add the squeezed-out marrow slices and the scooped-out interiors you have kept. Bring to the boil, add the cucumber purée, ½ pint (300 ml) cucumber juice and dill. Bring back to the boil and simmer, stirring occasionally, for 10–15 minutes.

Before serving, assess whether the texture is too liquid: it should have the consistency of a very thick sauce. If it is not thick enough, mix the soured cream thoroughly with the flour in a bowl, add 2–3 ladles of the marrow liquid gradually until absolutely smooth and gradually stir into the marrow. If, however, the texture is already thick enough, do not add the flour, but go through the same procedure to blend in the soured cream. Bring back to the boil and remove.

It must not be overcooked, as you will be left with porridge consistency. The marrow must stay fairly firm. Serve at the table from a large, preferably covered, vegetable dish or casserole.

It is a wonderfully flavoured, substantial accompaniment to be served with simply cooked meat. It goes better with the lighter kind, such as veal or a roast bird. Beef will overpower it.

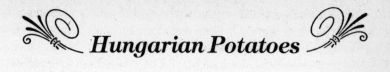

Hungarian Potatoes

Many people today hardly remember — or if they do it is only from their early childhood — the days of austerity when weekly family food budgets were a widespread problem. This potato dish takes me back to meatless days during the siege of Budapest, when it fulfilled a really useful purpose because it could — and certainly still can — be eaten as a main course. Vegetarians please note.

The simpler the dish, the more important it is to be meticulous about details: with care you may turn it into a delicacy. Thus the variety of potatoes you use should not be finally chosen until you have experimented — the ingredients are cheap enough. You should aim at the kind with low fat content which will more readily soak up the sauce. Forget about new potatoes, and make sure the ones you choose are not too small. Though I say 'cubes' on the page overleaf, the important thing is that their length should not exceed about 1½".

In the cooking process, the potatoes tend to break up and some no doubt will. Personally, I welcome this, as the somewhat — but not entirely — 'mashed' consistency also soaks up the wonderful paprika juices more easily. At any rate, the potatoes should fall to pieces in your mouth — if you have to use your teeth, even to the smallest degree, the dish has failed.

I implore you to choose the right kind of paprika, sold in small bags and clearly marked 'sweet noble' or, if it happens to come from Hungary, 'édes nemes'. It is, indeed, sweet and noble, almost devoid of sharpness, and keeps its vivid red colour provided you do not heat it until it has been mixed with at least a modicum of liquid. By all means, use any other kind of hot red pepper, but don't blame me for an inedible, unpleasantly hot mess.

HUNGARIAN POTATOES

Serves 4

3 lb (1.3 kg) potatoes (not new
 potatoes)
1 small or half a medium onion
1½ oz (40 g) lard or 1½ fl. oz (40 ml)
 cooking oil
3 level teaspoons 'sweet noble' (not
 hot) paprika

1 medium clove garlic
Pinch of caraway seeds
¾–1 pint (450–600 ml) stock
Salt and pepper

Peel the potatoes and cut them into 1–1½" cubes. Finely chop the onion. Heat the lard or oil in a saucepan. Add the chopped onion and cook until it turns light brown. Add the paprika, remove immediately from the heat (paprika turns black very fast) and stir thoroughly.

Add the potatoes, return to the heat and cook for 1–2 minutes, constantly stirring. Crush or finely chop the garlic and add to the potatoes, together with the caraway seeds. Top up with stock or water, its level should not quite cover the potatoes. Bring to the boil, add salt and pepper to taste, then keep cooking at a fairly low heat (do not cover) for about 15 minutes.

The cooking time depends on the kind of potatoes you use, but the aim is to keep as many of the potato cubes whole as possible. Nearly all the cooking juice should have evaporated and you should be left with a small quantity of very thick sauce. Don't worry if some of the potatoes break up and look mashed — it will even improve the taste.

This is a splendid accompaniment to sausages, but can also enliven a plate of otherwise dull meat.

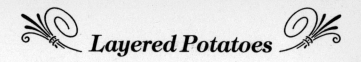

Layered Potatoes

Apart from supplanting many old, traditional favourites, nouvelle cuisine has also ruined simple vegetables, by moussifying them mercilessly. As if we were all toothless! Substantial side dishes of old have fared even worse and seem to have disappeared: what happened to cauliflower gratiné, broccoli topped with Hollandaise sauce, the rice-and-green peas mélange, perhaps with a little chopped mushrooms, we used to call rizzi-bizzi? They used to complement so aptly the lighter and more modest main courses, like grilled paillard of veal, or devilled chicken, and injected a great deal of interest into a simple meal.

Although practically unknown in Britain, layered potatoes illustrate my point well. They are in fact so substantial and succulent that they can stand in for a main course in their own right.

The version on the page overleaf can be adapted. Turn it into a substantial dish by using smoked cooking sausage instead of bacon, plenty of it, cut into thin rings. *Salade frisée* served with it, after, say, a mushroom soup (see page 17), and to round it off fresh fruit salad or perhaps pears poached in red wine with a little cream, make this unusual dish the centre of a minor country feast when accompanied by a white wine of substance, such as a Condrieu or a Graves.

LAYERED POTATOES

Serves 4–5

*5 lb (2.2 kg) potatoes (not new
  potatoes)*
3 eggs
3 rashers smoked streaky bacon
½ pint (300 ml) soured cream

1 level teaspoon salt
*Some butter for buttering a
  casserole*
*3 tablespoons light-coloured
  breadcrumbs*

Peel the potatoes and cut into ⅓″ thick slices. Hard-boil the eggs, shell and cut into rings with an egg slicer. Cut the bacon rashers into ¼″ pieces.

Cook the potatoes in boiling water for 7–8 minutes. Place the soured cream in a mixing bowl, add salt, then the potato slices and thoroughly but carefully coat with soured cream, without breaking them up.

Butter the bottom and sides of a casserole which is not too tall. Line bottom with a layer of potatoes, lightly sprinkle with some of the bacon, add a layer of a few egg slices, then a potato layer, followed by a sprinkling of bacon, then an egg layer and so on, finishing with a potato layer. Sprinkle the top with breadcrumbs. Cook on the top shelf of the oven (so as to ensure browning) at 220°C (425°F) or gas mark 7, until the top is well browned (about 20 minutes).

This goes well with grilled meat, particularly veal or pork, but it is quite a satisfying dish as a main course on its own, for example for a light, late supper.

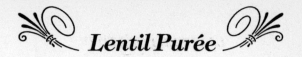

Lentil Purée

After the siege of Budapest, when the Hungarian provisional govern-ment was still 250 miles to the East, well behind the Russian troops, I was flabbergasted by a letter brought by messenger and signed by the provisional Minister of Food. It commissioned me, the acting head of my father's several restaurants and only in my twenties, to organise the feed-ing of the numerous members of all three Military Control Commissions, including the highest ranking officers. And food was, of course, very scarce in the city.

The President of the Republic was installed informally and as yet without proper entertaining facilities, landing me with yet more problems. He started to give state banquets, for some 24 guests each — the first one, of course, for the Russian military high command. I had no idea who would be there and was overawed to be hovering in the dining room around guests who included Voroshilov, Gromyko, who was then a political adviser, and Stalin's son, an air force officer attached to the Military Commission.

Meat was easily requisitioned by the Russians for my staff. In my quest for the best wines of the country (our own restaurant cellars had been plundered by the retreating Germans), I discovered some that had been walled in during the war. Keen to show off my treasure trove complete with its tell-tale dust, I ordered the bottles to be placed on the table, corks drawn but otherwise untouched. I was horrified to find on entering the dining room that some batman assigned to the President had polished every bottle as assiduously as his own army boots!

Meanwhile the population had to rely on such things as potatoes, beans and lentils, the latter in particularly ample supply. Mind you, those lentils were nothing to be ashamed of, prepared as they were with considerable panache, so much so that in spite of all that requisitioned food at my command, I still partook in the occasional bowl of lentils — and still serve them frequently, particularly with game, in purée form.

LENTIL PURÉE

Serves 6

10 oz (300 g) brown lentils
1 pint (600 ml) chicken stock (cubes will do)
1 teaspoon dry sherry
1 teaspoon brown vermouth
1 teaspoon sherry vinegar
3 bayleaves

2 or 3 pieces of thinly pared lemon rind
1 medium clove garlic, finely chopped
1 teaspoon salt
¼ teaspoon freshly ground pepper
7 fl oz (200 ml) soured cream

Soak the lentils in cold water for at least 8–10 hours, then drain.

Bring the chicken stock to the boil, add the lentils and all other ingredients, except the soured cream. Simmer until the stock is almost — but not quite — absorbed. Remove the lemon rind and bayleaves. Purée the lentils in a blender thoroughly and adjust the consistency, if necessary, with a little chicken stock (the purée should be thick). Mix in the soured cream, heat and serve. (To achieve a very smooth result, it is best to pass the puréed lentils through a sieve before reheating and adding the soured cream.)

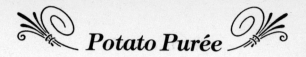

Potato Purée

Cigar smokers are not born; they are made and developed. They start with Manikins, then they may go on to Jamaican cigars and could eventually take to Havanas. And there is progression even in Havanas: you may start with the light Rey del Mundo, then progress to Bolivar before perhaps acquiring a taste for large Upmanns.

Potato purée is a somewhat similar taste. The lowest form of its life is mash (as in 'sausages and mash'), when potatoes are boiled in salted water and simply broken up with a masher. There is nothing wrong with that, provided that you choose potatoes with a reasonable — but not too great — fat content. The next step up is the same form with a little butter, a pinch each of ground black pepper and, according to taste, ground nutmeg.

That's the point at which you graduate to the use of the so-called potato ricer, a metal contraption through which you press the well-boiled potatoes so they come out in long rice form. They can then be turned into potato purée by bringing the result to the boil with milk and butter while mixing them forcefully with a wooden spoon. Embellishments are in order: I like to beat yolks of egg into them (three for six people) just before serving. Others (not I) add a pinch or two of ground nutmeg. Much depends on the potatoes: they should be low in fat content (you are adding milk and butter anyhow). Be warned against the use of a food blender — it turns the purée sticky and gluey. (See page 163 for an intriguing variety.)

You can go further still. The key is a fine-mesh sieve, the one stretched inside the top of a wooden drum. You have to use a pestle which is in the shape of a wide-bottomed mushroom. And at that point we arrive to the purée's highest form of life: Joel Robuchon's *purée de pommes de terre*. Here is his recipe. To have it at his restaurant — recognised for the best cooking in Paris — is a most surprising experience. You never knew that anything like it existed. As I once wrote, Robuchon uses potato purée as an art form. He should really call it something else.

POTATO PURÉE

Serves 6
The secret of this dish is to pass the potatoes three times through a very
fine sieve of the kind described on the previous page; twice before the
butter is added and again after adding the warmed milk.

2¼lb (1 kg) good boiling potatoes   7 fl oz (200 ml) milk, warmed
   (such as Maris Piper or Cara)   Salt
9 oz (250 g) butter, diced

Peel the potatoes and shape them so that they are all the same size to
ensure even cooking.

Cover with cold water, bring to a boil and cook for 20 minutes or until
they are tender when pierced with a knife. Drain and pass *twice* through a
fine sieve into the saucepan.

Dry over a low heat, stirring constantly with a wooden spoon. Add the
butter, stirring vigorously. It is important to mix it well to make it elastic
again.

Gradually add the warmed milk. Check the seasoning and pass the
purée through a fine sieve again. Re-heat but do not bring to the boil.

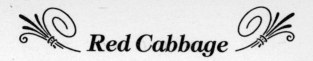

Red Cabbage

Few dishes are raped more disgracefully in myriad kitchens than red cabbage. It is a wonderful, aromatic, piquant accompanying dish — at any rate the one described overleaf is. Yet so many times on my restaurant plate it has been dark, almost black, either unforgivably bland and used as a mere blob of colour to contrast with something or other, or far too acidic — and almost always as part of a selection of other garnishes, an apology for the lack of imagination.

It should play a character part without upstaging a dramatic protagonist such as game, although in its acid corruption that is precisely what it would do. Nor should it he humiliated and reduced to the role of a clown — a fate it suffers when added, cold, to a salad. Properly made, nothing does more justice to the best saddle of venison or to a venison steak. Excellent with the creamy, continental variety of saddle of hare, its slight vinegar content, perhaps fractionally increased for the important occasion, helps this rich dish and, by the way, the digestion as well.

It loyally springs into action when the main role is played by lesser stars, such as a succulent steak. But it really shines and comes into its own when it forms part of a court, perhaps together with pears poached in red wine or apples in white, paying homage to such princes of the table as roast goose or sucking pig. Without its support, even they would make a lesser impression.

RED CABBAGE

Serves 6
It is preferable to prepare this dish a day in advance.

1 medium red cabbage
4 fl oz (100 ml) olive oil
2 level teaspoons caraway seeds
2 medium cloves garlic, finely
   chopped
1 piece thinly pared lemon peel
2 level teaspoons salt

Freshly ground pepper (6–7 turns of
   the pepper mill)
1 bottle dry white wine
1½ level tablespoons granulated
   sugar
1–1½ fl oz (30–40 ml) white wine
   vinegar

Discard the single, outer layer of the red cabbage. Cut the red cabbage in two halves, then cut away and discard the white core at the bottom.

On a wooden slicer (called a mandolin), shred each half into ⅛–¼" thick shavings. With a large carving knife, slice the bits you cannot put through the mandolin, and the left-overs, into shreds of approximately the same thickness — the longer the better.

Heat the oil in a saucepan, add the shredded red cabbage, stir thoroughly, cover and keep cooking for 3–4 minutes on fairly high heat, until it is well heated through. Add the caraway seeds, finely chopped garlic, lemon peel, salt and pepper. Then keep stirring every half minute or so for 5 minutes.

Add the wine, sugar and vinegar. Bring to the boil, then turn the heat down, half-cover the saucepan so there is room for the liquid to evaporate, and continue cooking at medium heat for about 40 minutes. If the wine evaporates completely before the cooking is finished (because the cabbage was fairly large), keep topping it up with a very little water from time to time, so as to arrive at a moist finish with just a minimum quantity of liquid at the bottom.

It is important to taste it just before the end of the cooking and adjust the flavour, mainly with vinegar and sugar and perhaps salt.

Sauerkraut in Champagne

Weekends are prime time for sauerkraut in our home, by force of circumstances, as I shall explain. But I am not complaining — quite the contrary. It is one of the most useful items in our food store, tins and tins of it (whatever that revelation may do to my reputation for truffles and caviar), because it lends itself to being elevated into something really worthwhile.

In a household as informal as ours the number of people who come for lunch on Sunday (by far the best time) or Saturday can sometimes be a stop-press decision. 'Do you mind terribly if we bring the kids/the youngsters/my parents?', the call may come on Saturday morning. I clap my hand over the receiver ... Barbara mimics with her upturned hands 'What are we giving them?' ... I whisper 'Sauerkraut' and laugh into the receiver: 'Of course, you must!' Out comes something or other from the freezer — pheasants or a gammon Barbara has smoked all day in the garden a few weeks before — otherwise we might manage some leg of pork from an excellent village butcher just before closing, the basis for a last-minute decision, or perhaps one or two free-range ducks for the oven. We are not only saved but will shine as well.

Or it could happen that just the two of us at dinner can only manage bockwurst (a spicier and longer version of frankfurters), excellent with mashed potatoes and this version of sauerkraut. It turns the pedestrian, German peasant sausage into something fit for French aristocrats.

To come back to the unexpected youngsters, the order of the day would be a mound of this special sauerkraut, topped, higgledy-piggledy, with all manner of goodies, such as boned knuckle of pork, double-thick rashers of bacon, loin of pork, rings of cooking sausage, all strictly smoked and, of course, boiled, together with two or three frankfurters cut lengthwise in half and lightly fried in a minimum of oil. Make no mistake: this is more than a stopgap. It's a veritable feast.

SAUERKRAUT IN CHAMPAGNE

Serves 6–8

2 x 2 lb (900g) tins sauerkraut
1 bottle Champagne and ½ bottle
   good white Burgundy
4 large pieces of thinly pared lemon
   rind
7–8 peppercorns

6–8 juniper berries
3 bayleaves
½ teaspoon salt
1 teaspoon sugar
½ medium clove garlic, finely
   chopped

Turn the contents of the sauerkraut tins into a large bowl of cold water and wash, then squeeze dry with your hands. (The thoroughness of washing will depend on the degree of acidity in the sauerkraut, but a very slight acidity should be retained.)

Now place the sauerkraut into a saucepan. Add the Champagne, white wine and all the other ingredients. Bring to the boil and cook at a medium heat, stirring a few times, until the liquid evaporates so the sauerkraut remains just moist.

Remove the lemon rind, bayleaves and those juniper berries that can easily be found (don't worry about leaving in a few).

This sauerkraut dish is ideal for a choucroute-type dish, i.e. heaped on to a large plate and topped with boiled, smoked meats (see previous page).

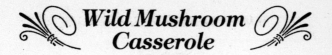 *Wild Mushroom Casserole*

The reason for the profusion of stunning and artistic pictures in the cookery books of recent years is the difficulty of reproducing these fanciful *nouvelle cuisine* dishes at home; so they must be illustrated. Such pictures, however, are daunting to the family cook, who is then reduced to voyeurism. The images may be thrilling, but their practical advantage is minimal. Does anyone ever manage these awesome creations at home?

Certain French guidebooks have a lot to answer for. They have led the ever credulous public to believe that taste and flavour no longer reign supreme and have to share the limelight, with the artistic image overshadowing old culinary values. The quest for visual art in French cuisine is on.

The effect of all this has been to diminish admiration for dishes that, to me, are still at the pinnacle. You are a fuddy-duddy if you rave about the duck *Rouennaise* at the Tour d'Argent, and downright anti-social to have two helpings (the leg is crisped while you enjoy the pink breast first). And what about the ethereal soufflé of frogs' legs when Oliver was still in harness at the Grand Véfour, or the calf's kidneys with two feather-light sauces when Lapérouse was still at the top? Not to mention the real *andouillette* you could discover only in tiny bistros (and of which, I am afraid, the legendary Hériot, Mayor of Lyon, once said: 'It is no good unless it smells of piss'). Such delights are a far cry from baby mousses, the excommunication of flour and the marriage of basically incompatible constituents just *pour épater les bourgeois*.

Thank goodness for the Bernard Pacauds of this world. At l'Ambrosisie, in the beautiful Place des Vosges (the last Paris restaurant to gain, in 1988, its third Michelin star), Pacaud respects his traditional roots without being a stick-in-the-mud: witness this casserole of wild mushrooms. Finding the right wild mushrooms might not be easy, but the quest for any flavoursome kind is worth it. Supermarkets have woken up — and if yours hasn't it is worth experimenting with dried ones.

WILD MUSHROOM CASSEROLE

Serves 6–8

5 lb (2.2 kg) wild mushrooms according to availability, but preferably to include the following: fresh morels, gyromites, petites pleurotes de souche, mousserons (meadow mushrooms or blewits) and petits cèpes (boletus mushrooms)
4 oz (100 g) butter

6 shallots, chopped
1/4 pint (500 ml) jellied stock (or tinned beef consommé)
2 1/2 pints (1.4 l) double cream
Salt
Mixed spices (2 cloves, 1 star aniseed, 1 tablespoon coriander, 1 tablespoon black pepper) roughly chopped and wrapped in muslin

Trim and wash all the mushrooms and blanch them in boiling salted water for 2–3 minutes. Drain well but do not cool.

Heat the butter in a large sauteuse or wide-based, large saucepan. Add the chopped shallots and allow to sweat, then add the stock and reduce to a glaze. Add the mushrooms and leave to stew over a gentle heat for 15 minutes. Add the double cream, a level teaspoon of salt and the spices in a muslin bag and stir well. Bring to the boil, skim the surface and transfer to a casserole dish. Cover and cook in a pre-heated oven at 180°C (350°F) or gas mark 4 for three hours. It can be served in individual dishes.

Desserts

Apple and Almond Pudding

When, on a Saturday afternoon, it suddenly turns out that we shall be eight, not four, for Sunday lunch, one of the panic questions is how to supplement the chocolate cake (or whatever) already prepared. That's when Barbara pulls one of her magic reserve ideas out of a hat. This is one of them: easy to prepare and quick (except for peeling, coring and slicing the apples), it is always a success.

However 'nice' apple desserts may be, they do tend to be on the dull side, even when a lot of trouble is taken. Take apple flans. Thin layer of apricot jam, wonderful, crumbly flan pastry and splendidly executed glazing: and yet the apples are still like mutton dressed up as lamb, notwithstanding the candied cherries added in the hope of a miracle. To me apple desserts remain an excuse for putting surplus apples to some supposedly sophisticated use. I may waver in my opinion in the case of apple pie, provided it contains some walnuts and a little cinnamon, but how often do you come across a really *good* apple pie?

Now Barbara's apple confection is in a different category, different because of the almond sponge which lifts apples to the level of refinement. Mind you, it's nothing much to look at — just a plain, browned top in a soufflé dish — so it is not only for taste, but also for appearance that you do need some rich, thick, preferably Jersey cream to flank it, half-moon shape, on the plate.

I am afraid I find raw apples pedestrian, too, except Cox's around Christmas when they are ripe, so the pips can be heard rattling inside when you shake them. Have you ever tried them with a piece of mild Cheddar or Emmenthal?

APPLE AND ALMOND PUDDING

Serves 6

4lb (1.8kg) eating apples	*4oz (100g) caster sugar*
2oz (50g) soft brown sugar	*2 eggs, lightly beaten*
5oz (150g) butter	*½ teaspoon almond essence*
2oz (50g) raisins	*4oz (100g) ground almonds*

Peel and cut up the apples, each into eight segments. Place in a saucepan with 1 tablespoon of water, the brown sugar, 1 oz (25 g) of the butter and stew until soft. Remove from the heat and add the raisins.

Pre-heat the oven to 170°C (350°F) or gas mark 4. Butter a deep pie dish, line the bottom with the stewed apple mixture and smooth the surface. In a mixing bowl, cream the remaining butter and caster sugar until pale, then beat in the eggs, a little at a time. Add, while mixing, the almond essence and ground almonds.

Spread this mixture over the apples in the pie dish: making the surface even with the back of a spoon. Bake in the pre-heated oven for about 1 hour until the surface appears a light golden brown.

Serve hot or cold, with whipped double cream.

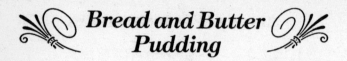

Bread and Butter Pudding

Curiously, bread and butter pudding has become something of a symbol of the revivalist trend in traditional British cooking. Perhaps Anton Mosimann has had something to do with it, his version having been demonstrated to five or six million viewers of the TV *Food & Drink* programme in a charming scene in which he cooked for a lorry driver's family in their kitchen in Sheffield. Another great chef, Michcl Bourdin of the Connaught Hotel, features it as a speciality of the house. His is said to be the best in London.

'In London' is right, because the very best in the British Isles is certainly Francis Coulson's at the Sharrow Bay, Ullswater, a splendid country house hotel in the Lake District. There is nobody whose hand is lighter and more adept with pastry and other desserts. Nobody could have paid him a greater compliment than chef Frédy Girardet in Switzerland, most highly respected by his peers the world over, who asked me to send him three recipes for bread and butter pudding and selected — and still uses — Francis Coulson's! A further proof: the syllabub Coulson prepared at Maxim's many years ago in the company of other eminent British chefs I took over to Paris, brought the house down. The French were puzzled by what they perceived to be an outlandish concoction, but, on the day, it amounted to their gastronomic Waterloo.

The merit of Coulson's bread and butter pudding is its exceptional lightness. Similar versions are heavier nearly everywhere.

BREAD AND BUTTER PUDDING

Serves 4–6

3 eggs
4oz (100g) sugar
9fl oz (250ml) milk
9fl oz (250ml) double cream
1 vanilla pod
3 drops vanilla essence
1½oz (40g) unsalted butter
3–4oz (75–100g) white bread or
  brioche

½lb (225g) sultanas, placed in
  boiling water to swell
Mixed spice
A little icing sugar
1lb (450g) tin apricots
1 tablespoon apricot jam
1 tablespoon apricot brandy
1 tablespoon chopped angelica

Mix the eggs and sugar together. Bring the milk, cream, vanilla pod and vanilla essence to the boil. Cool slightly and add the egg/sugar mixture. Pass through a sieve.

Have ready six large, individual ramekin dishes and butter them. Cut a circle of bread (or brioche) to fit the base of each ramekin. Sprinkle the swollen sultanas on the top of each. Cut the remaining bread (or brioche) into thin strips and arrange them in a lattice shape by criss-crossing them over the top of each filled ramekin. Pour the egg/cream mixture carefully over the layers until it reaches the rim of each dish. Top with a knob of butter and a little mixed spice.

Bake in a bain marie at 150°C (300°F) or gas mark 2 until set (about 35–40 minutes). Sprinkle the tops with icing sugar and put under the grill for a few minutes to glaze.

Serve with apricot sauce: Liquidise the apricots with a tablespoon of the apricot syrup and the apricot jam, heat with a little water and stir over the heat to a thick sauce consistency. Flavour, if you like, with a little apricot brandy and finely chopped angelica.

If you prefer a whole, single pudding, work accordingly.

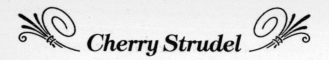

Cherry Strudel

They would, wouldn't they? I mean, the Austrians *would* say that strudel is Austrian. They are the culinary pirates of Europe. Most of the peoples of the old Austro-Hungarian empire had very individual national cuisines and some of their specialities inevitably drifted into the empire's capital, Vienna, where they were expropriated without scruple.

The secret of a superb strudel is the pastry. Today, a tremendous amount of drudgery is saved with reasonable filo pastry available in supermarkets, but nothing could replace the real thing which enterprising pâtisseries still make. That pastry, after careful assembling, resting and so on, is stretched over a very large kitchen table, covered with freshly laundered tablecloths, using the back of the hand closed in a fist, so that fingernails don't tear it. The laborious, delicate stretching goes on, the pastry showing miraculous elasticity, until it hangs almost to the floor from all four sides of the table and until it is so transparent (it used to be said semi-jokingly) that one could read a newspaper through it. That all-important elasticity comes from the high gluten content of wheat grown on special soil in a special climate, and no other flour except that grown on the Hungarian plains has it to the necessary degree (Canadian flour has somewhat similar properties). So the strudel's original home was not Austria.

Morello cherries, the other vital element, are again Hungarian produce, with a special kind of bitter-sweet taste that you don't come across in the fruit of other countries. The most famous is the Spanish variety, plump and very soft, but too acidic and juicy for the purpose. Let them concentrate on apple strudel in Austria, the king of strudels remains the one with cherry. It has individuality, an intriguing blend of flavours that the somewhat cloying *apfelstrudel* (ruined by the superfluous whipped cream) cannot match.

My two other favourites are poppyseed strudel and cabbage strudel, but that's another chapter — perhaps in another book.

CHERRY STRUDEL

Serves about 12

This can be prepared with ready-made filo pastry which is acceptable but freshly-made strudel pastry is much better. In this case use only flour with a high gluten content, e.g. Canadian or Hungarian flour. IT IS USELESS TO ATTEMPT IT WITH ORDINARY FLOUR.

For the pastry
10oz (300g) flour
1 egg yolk
A few drops wine vinegar
4oz (100g) lard, melted
1oz (25g) icing sugar

For the filling
¹/₂oz (15g) sultanas
2lb (900g) stoned morello cherries,
*   fresh or from a tin*
2oz (50g) white fresh breadcrumbs
4oz (100g) icing sugar
1 level teaspoon ground cinnamon
4oz (100g) ground walnuts

Soak the sultanas in luke warm water.

Make a softer than usual dough: sift the flour into a heap on a working surface and place the yolk, vinegar and 1¹/₂ tablespoons melted lard in the middle. Work this into a fairly soft dough, if necessary controlling the consistency with the addition of roughly 4fl oz (100ml) water. It will be ready when none of it sticks to your fingers or the working surface, and the dough starts breaking out in blisters. Brush this all over with ¹/₂ teaspoon of melted lard, cover and keep in a warm place for about 30 minutes.

Meanwhile prepare filling: drain the morello cherries thoroughly, keep them whole and mix with all the other ingredients, including the swollen — but drained — sultanas.

While the dough is still resting, cover a table, about 3 x 2 feet, with a clean tablecloth. Flour the tablecloth lightly with the palm of your hand and smooth it out. Place the rested dough in the middle and start stretching it in all directions, but *only with the back of both your clenched fists, never with your fingers or the palm of your hand* so that no tear is caused. It should be stretched until it is very thin indeed and hangs down from all four edges of the table. If you find that you don't succeed the first time and there are tears in the thin pastry, gather it all up, form a dough again and start from the beginning. (You will not succeed if the flour has not got a high enough gluten content.) When this has been achieved, cut off the bits of pastry hanging from the table with a pair of scissors.

Do not leave the stretched pastry to dry for more than a minute or two as it will start cracking. Sprinkle it lightly with 1½ tablespoons of melted lard. Spread the filling carefully, lightly (without pressure) and evenly all over the pastry.

Start rolling the strudel: along one of the longer sides of the table, cover the edge of the spread with the overlap of the stretched dough to the width of about 1½–2″. Now get hold of the tablecloth with both hands on one of the two longer sides of the table and roll the pastry with the filling like a Swiss roll by very slowly lifting the cloth vertically. This will let the pastry roll naturally, without the help of your bare hands. Now and again pull the cloth horizontally towards you and continue rolling by again lifting the cloth vertically, as before, until a long roll has been formed.

Grease a baking tray with ½ teaspoon of melted lard and cut the rolled strudel into lengths to fit the tray. Sprinkle with the remaining melted lard (approximately 1½ tablespoons). Bake in an oven preheated to 180°C (350°F) or gas mark 4 until the covering pastry is brown. Serve either hot or cold. Sprinkle with icing sugar from a sifter before serving.

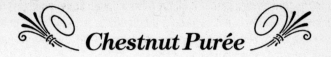

Chestnut Purée

I instantly associate chestnuts, though not in their sweetened form, with skating. It brings back crisp, continental winters with severely freezing but invigorating temperatures. Shawl-wrapped, red-nosed women sat on stools at street corners, bending over their little round, open ovens and ministering to the slit-shelled chestnuts with their hands, except for the fingers, covered by black woollen gloves. The charcoal glowed cheeringly and invitingly through the grates and the cry was: 'Roast chestnuts, warm chestnuts please!' Unable to resist, we warmed our hands on the large, thin paper cones filled with the crunchy, charred yet tender substances before peeling and letting them gently crumble in our mouths. Bliss.

Chestnuts, of course, had other uses. Pâtisseries, apart from being hiding places with teenage girlfriends to escape their chaperones, displayed tempting concoctions to make your mouth water. We filled our plates with millefeuille layered with *crème pâtissière*; large, featherlight éclairs, 'punch' slices sprinkled with rum, umpteen kinds of chocolate gâteaux; and much else. But the star turn was chestnut purée. It had been squeezed through a so-called potato ricer onto amazingly light whipped cream, the secret being a special machine aerating the cream while whipping it. No sugar, since that went into the purée made of chestnuts that had been cooked together with split vanilla sticks. After it had been forced through a fine sieve and kneaded with sugar, a little deep-brown rum clinched it.

Then there were gâteaux layered with light chocolate sponge and chestnut butter cream, covered with chocolate, or, to end all gâteaux, the miraculous chestnut croque-en-bouche, a very tall edifice built entirely of large bonbon-shaped chestnut balls dipped in dark chocolate, the whole thing lightly shrouded with spun sugar. Sensuous.

Why do we make so little of our chestnut opportunities in this country?

CHESTNUT PURÉE

Serves 4

For this dish you need a so-called potato ricer, which is a two-handled utensil for mashing and squeezing through cooked potatoes, spaghetti-shaped.

1 lb (450g) tin chestnut purée
(unsweetened)
¼lb (100g) caster sugar
½ teaspoon vanilla essence

3 teaspoons rum
½ pint (300ml) whipping cream
Optional: icing sugar

Mix the chestnut purée, sugar, vanilla essence and rum very thoroughly in a mixing bowl with your hand. Adjust the quantity of sugar to taste. Fill the potato ricer with this mixture and place what is left over on a plate. Keep on the bottom shelf of the refrigerator for at least 30–40 minutes before serving to firm up the mixture before squeezing it through the ricer.

Just before serving, whip the cream to a fairly firm texture, scoop it on to a large, round serving dish and mould it into a conical shape, or pipe it on to the dish with a piping bag to the same shape.

Hold the potato ricer high over the whipped cream and press the chestnut through, so that it 'rains' down, spaghetti shaped, on to the whipped cream. You can, if you have a really sweet tooth, sprinkle a very little icing sugar on the top sparingly with a sugar sifter, but you must do so immediately before serving otherwise the sugar will melt.

Christmas Pudding

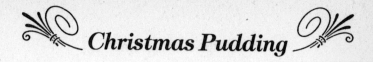

Continentals don't understand English puddings. It is one of the reasons why their annoying haughtiness towards English cooking, now quite out of date, still persists. It is the British who are the real connoisseurs of the last course. While continentals just pick at something prettily presented, the course. While continentals just pick at something prettily presented, the British rightly consider it as an important part of the meal, and never mind the looks — let's get down to it (except those who fall for the claptrap of 'experts' conspiring with doctors, who terrorise worried eaters). They don't know what they are missing in Europe. Well, perhaps after 1992... Spotted Dick, suet pudding, treacle tart, Christmas pudding — here we come!

Special prejudice is reserved for Christmas pudding, yet I cannot understand how anyone approaching good food with gusto can fail to appreciate it. There are so many facets to it: the scrumptious texture that suet lends has an instant impact on the palate; its richness is intriguingly spicy; innumerable flavours blend into a new one through months of storing.

It was years ago when I was sent a Christmas pudding in a PR exercise, with the recipe printed on the side of a pudding basin. Guinness was, of course, included, but I confess it was news to me then. Barbara, who has adapted the Guinness recipe, wouldn't dream of leaving it out. I have no idea what it does to the pudding, but it works splendidly.

Personally, I am not a brandy sauce man. And I am puzzled when my wife, and most of our guests, treble the indulgence by soaking the pudding in thick cream. So, at the Christmas dinner, there is a special little sauce boat for me with apricot sauce which I make simply by heating apricot jam with about one-fifth water and when it boils I add brown rum, its quantity equalling that of the water. Every time there are converts — very appropriate at Christmas.

CHRISTMAS PUDDING

Each pudding serves 6
(One can be kept for the following year)

*8oz (225g) fresh white
  breadcrumbs
8oz (225g) soft brown sugar
8oz (225g) currants
10oz (300g) chopped raisins
8oz (225g) sultanas
2oz (50g) chopped mixed peel
10oz (300g) shredded suet*

*1 teaspoon mixed spice
½ teaspoon salt
Grated rind of 1 lemon
1 dessertspoon lemon juice
2 large eggs, beaten
¼ pint (150ml) milk
½ pint (275ml) Guinness*

Thoroughly grease two 6½" pudding basins.

Mix all the dry ingredients together in a large bowl. Stir in the lemon juice, eggs, milk and Guinness, mix well and turn into the pudding basins.

Cover each basin with a layer of greaseproof paper followed by a layer of foil; trim and secure well with string.

Leave overnight.

The following day, steam the puddings in a covered saucepan (or two saucepans) for 7½ hours, making sure the saucepan does not boil dry.

Turn the puddings out and serve. If not eaten immediately, they can be reheated by steaming before serving.

The puddings can be stored for up to one year in the sealed cooking basin.

Coffee Granita

There is a time and place for everything. For coffee granita, as far as I am concerned, it is around 4 p.m. on the piazza of the Isle of Capri.

Fleeting visitors to Capri never understand my enthusiasm for the world's most beautiful island, because it wasn't meant for day-trippers. When the boats start disgorging them at 11 a.m., every self-respecting, longer-term visitor is already on one of the half a dozen rock beaches, perhaps the late Gracie Fields' Canzone del Mare, or the one overlooking the Faraglione, a gorgeous rock formation in a heavenly, miniature bay. The sun is enervating, the intermittent showers reviving, the bitter Carpano vermouth is on the rocks. The sea is velvet; the salad, assembled from shellfish caught the same morning, tastes of the sea. Time has no meaning. Watches are unused. You take your cue from the progress of the sun — when it's nearing the horizon, you catch the bus that takes only three to four minutes to roar through the hairpin bends of the precipitous road to the piazza.

The day-trippers have left and you squeeze on to a large but crowded terrace. *Far' niente*, except to look at the stunning shapes of deep-tanned girls, or to avert your eyes when a fat, silk-shirted tycoon, possibly with a yacht in the harbour, wanders into view. And you order *granita di caffé*, a bitter-sweet, ice-cold stimulant. Chances are that you return to the same terrace late after dinner to be part of a stage setting with the squat church tower, 50 yards away, rising against a navy blue sky and the clock-tower bell on the edge of the terrace tolling sonorously every 15 minutes.

The coffee granita of Simon Hopkinson at the Bibendum restaurant in London, surpasses even that in Capri.

COFFEE GRANITA

Serves 8

Dark-roast beans must be used for this recipe. Ideally it should be
espresso coffee. Do not use instant coffee.

2 pints (1.1 litre), treble *strength*   *8oz (225g) caster sugar*
     coffee

Dissolve the sugar thoroughly in the coffee. Cool the mixture.

Pour into a shallow tray suitable for the freezer. Place in the freezer and
leave until it begins to set around the edges.

Every 20 minutes run a fork through the mixture. The aim is eventually
to develop a consistency of loose crushed ice. Once this is achieved, the
granita is ready to be served as a dessert.

It should be served in wine glasses wide at the top, but individual glass
bowls will do. It goes well with cream not too firmly whipped and placed on
top immediately before serving to preserve its texture.

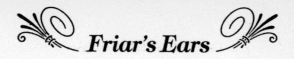

Friar's Ears

I am all for unusual names given to good dishes partly for fun, partly to intrigue and tempt. Consider what Spotted Dick and Roly Poly have done for marvellous English puddings, and how much Hot Cross Buns have added to the coffers of bakeries. Beef Wellington may have soothed the hurt pride of the French (insensitively enough I once presented it at a lunch of l'Académie des Gastronomes in Paris, and I wasn't expelled).

Misleading names are another matter. 'Farm fresh', 'morning gathered' and similar embarrassing nonsenses have almost disappeared, but 'Aylesbury duckling' (possibly from East Anglia), 'Scottish salmon' (most probably from a fish 'farm' in the South), or 'Welsh lamb' (often from Devon) are examples of what is still a widespread practice. Nor will the name 'Caspian canapé' change the country of origin from Denmark to Russia.

Which brings me to a friend of mine, a young member of an ancient aristocratic family in Hungary, who emigrated penniless to the West and was constantly and lavishly entertained thanks to family connections. At one point he was given a case of Champagne, which enabled him at last to return lots of hospitality. *Noblesse oblige*, so he prepared his version of caviar canapés by slightly cooking semolina, adding puréed anchovies and completing the disguise with some tablets containing medicinal charcoal, a harmless dye but also a mild laxative. The canapés looked — even tasted somewhat — like the real thing, but I have not been told whether the guests had any after thoughts.

So what's in a name? Could 'Friar's Ears', the marvellous pasta which you eat as a dessert, indicate the shape? Or might it reflect the fact that some monasteries in pre-war Hungary couldn't resist temptation of the flesh when it amounted to succulent food? Or was it christened thus just for fun?

FRIAR'S EARS

Serves 6

8–10 oz (225–300g) plum jam (only
    the thickest, most dense jam will
    do)
1 level teaspoon ground cinnamon
5 oz (150g) caster sugar

3 eggs
1 lb (450g) semolina flour
3 oz (75g) fresh white breadcrumbs
3 oz (75g) butter
4 oz (100g) finely ground walnuts

Make the filling: mix the plum jam, cinnamon and 1 oz (25 g) caster sugar.

Prepare the pasta: break the eggs and beat them lightly with a fork to blend the yolks and whites. Sift the flour, add three-quarters of the beaten eggs and work into a fairly stiff dough while adding water gradually to achieve the required texture. Divide this mixture into two or three parts and roll them, one by one, with a rolling pin on a floured surface, into very thin sheets.

Take one sheet and place on it blobs of the plum jam mixture, 1 teaspoonful each, about 2½″ distant from each other, so they are in the middle of 2½″ squares. Use some of the remaining beaten eggs to brush ½″ thick dividing lines between them, horizontally and vertically. Now place another sheet of pasta of equal size on top and press down hard along all the lines you have drawn with the brush. Then cut along these lines with a pastry wheel, to obtain ravioli shapes. Repeat this with the other sheets until you have used all the plum jam mixture.

Place the filled pasta into boiling — but not fiercely boiling — water. When they come to the surface, drain them thoroughly in a sieve.

Brown the breadcrumbs in butter in a large sauteuse or large, shallow casserole dish. Add the filled pasta, carefully agitate the dish and turn the pasta with a large wooden spoon to coat them. Take care not to break them up.

Mix the finely ground walnuts and the remaining sugar. Serve the breadcrumb-coated pasta on large plates and sprinkle very generously with the sugar-and-walnut mixture.

(It may be useful to have some more finely ground walnuts and some more of the plum jam mixture ready for those with a sweet tooth who may want to help themselves to either or both.)

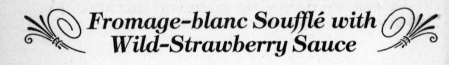

Fromage-blanc Soufflé with Wild-Strawberry Sauce

Is superb food the thing that makes a superb restaurant? Well, it isn't everything. Take a great theatrical evening: many factors, beyond an excellent play, go into the making of a memory.

If the restaurant doesn't have an immediate impact when you enter, the evening will never take off. Smoothness and style has to surround you instantly. A country hostelry, if it is well run, can be as stylish in its own way as a sophisticated and luxurious place. An imperceptible tension, too, has to be in the air, with a measure of expectation and restrained eagerness in the staff. It shows a strong, experienced hand behind the scenes. Laxity is the kiss of death.

Whatever impression *you* make on the staff, they must radiate deference tempered with dignity. You must be made to believe that they *care* about your wellbeing and that you are the centre of all their attention.

Then, absolute skill. Not necessarily a spectacular way with the duck press, but evidence of experience and unceasing practice behind the performance, for example, the way dishes are carried overhead in a crowded brasserie in Paris. Carelessness, let alone clumsiness, is also a kiss of death.

Elaborate china, glasses or linen are suspect; elegant simplicity is imperative. Colossal and colourful menus and wine lists are vulgar, yet there must be an *embarras de richesse* to make you feel spoilt. And there should be a maître d'hotel with the bearing of a toreador and the charm of a diplomat.

Come to think of it, I have almost exactly described the Auberge de l'Ill at Illhaeusern in Alsace. To describe the superiority of its soufflé dish would be much more difficult.

FROMAGE-BLANC SOUFFLÉ WITH WILD-STRAWBERRY SAUCE

Serves 6

Melted butter and caster sugar, for
    the moulds
4 egg yolks
5 oz (150 g) sugar
Grated rind of 1 lemon
Vanilla essence
6 oz (175 g) firm fromage blanc
    (available at Sainsbury's)

5 egg whites
3 oz (75 g) sultanas

For the sauce
½ lb (225 g) strawberries
    (preferably wild) or raspberries
4 oz (100 g) caster sugar
Juice of ½ lemon

Brush the ramekin dishes or individual moulds with melted butter and dust with sugar.

Whisk the egg yolks, 3 oz (75 g) sugar, the grated lemon rind and 1 or 2 drops of vanilla essence until thick and creamy. Add the fromage blanc.

Whisk the egg whites until they leave a peak adding 2 oz (50 g) of the sugar a little at a time. Fold the egg whites and sultanas into the egg yolk mixture with a spatula.

Fill the moulds with the soufflé mixture, smooth over the surface with a spatula and cook in a bain marie in a preheated oven at 180°C (350°C) or gas mark 4 for 20 minutes.

Meanwhile, make the sauce. Wipe the fruit clean. Put 4 oz (100 g) of the caster sugar into a saucepan, cover with 3½ fl oz (90 ml) water and bring to the boil. Boil for 3 minutes, remove the syrup from the heat and allow to cool a little. Purée the wild strawberries (or raspberries) in a blender and add the cooked syrup and the juice of half a freshly squeezed lemon. Pass the sauce through a sieve.

When the soufflés are cooked, let them stand for a few minutes before turning them out on to individual plates. Surround with the wild strawberry sauce.

Gemma's Almond Cake

There was a time when, for me, the Isle of Capri was the only conceivable place for a holiday. During the long English winters my thoughts were often with Gemma's Restaurant. Naturally, the first evening, and many subsequent ones, Barbara and I headed for it automatically.

Some restaurant interiors only work in a Mediterranean climate. Anywhere else Gemma's décor — pink-washed walls, sparsely covered here and there with wisteria, encased in metal-framed glass — would not have merited a second look. Yet it felt like being in the backyard of an Italian peasant house with its total informality and the absence of time and conventions. The air was redolent of good food, the provenance of the down-to-earth wine of no importance.

And, of course, there was dear old Gemma, with her whispy, grey-red hair, her red cardigan and black apron and her sincere Cheshire-cat smile. Apart from the packed room at the height of conviviality, the main draw was the skill of Gemma's sister in the kitchen. I treasure the memories of gnocchi, sea bass with fennel (why does it never taste the same in Britain?), and small veal escalopes with a delectable, thin lemon sauce. There was a most remarkable pizza, made in an old pizza oven without a door so that you could watch it swell and break out in bubbles next to the open wood fire.

Gemma's cakes, too, were good, none better than the *torta de mandela*, full of almond flavour and more moist than most cakes of that ilk. I offer this as a memorial to that unforgettable restaurateur.

GEMMA'S ALMOND CAKE

Serves 8

9 oz (250 g) caster sugar
5 oz (150 g) softened butter
5 large eggs, separated
9 oz (250 g) ground almonds
4 drops almond essence
5 oz (150 g) dark chocolate, grated or ground

2 tablespoons plain flour
1 teaspoon baking powder
Extra butter and flour for preparing the cake tin
Icing sugar for sifting

Work the sugar and butter together into a creamy texture. Add the egg yolks, one by one, while beating, then add the ground almonds, almond essence and the chocolate.

Beat the egg whites until stiff and gently fold into the cake mixture along with the flour and baking powder.

Butter and slightly flour the inside of an 8½" cake tin with a removable base. Turn the mixture into it and bake at 160°C (320°F) or gas mark 3 for about 1 hour, or until a skewer inserted into the centre comes out clean.

Remove from the oven and leave to cool. Place upside down on a serving dish, remove the tin and sprinkle generously with icing sugar before serving.

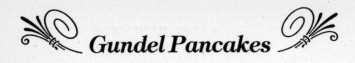

Gundel Pancakes

O h, the garden restaurants in old Budapest! They were very special and so different from those in other capitals.

The best-known in Paris is the stylish Pré Catalan in the Bois de Boulogne featuring *grande cuisine*. The clientèle doesn't arrive — it makes an appearance. At lunch the place becomes a summer annexe of downtown financial and oil company headquarters. If Parisians of 150 years ago arrived from their graves in powdered wigs, the formal waiters would cope without batting an eyelid.

In Rome the mood is warm. Large families celebrate something or other around tables for eight or 10, ties are the exception and earthy dishes reflect gusto and appetite.

In Vienna the garden restaurants are in Grinzing, a suburb, where every house seems to be one. Some of the 'gardens' are glorified courtyards, with new wine flowing and food reduced to sausage level, but the tone is just as *gemütlich* as if it were après-ski time. The sound of singsongs is drifting out from every doorway.

In old Budapest, garden restaurants were a microcosm. The procession started at 8.30 p.m.: attractive, shapely women most elegantly dressed (often by small and cheap dressmakers in small flats), with dashing young officers in tow; the rich and envied shopkeeper with his daughter and corpulent wife; the celebrated actress with her court; a dodgy politician or two expecting all the attention; two or three ingenious but impecunious authors attracting admiration; a general decorated like a Christmas tree; a well-known lawyer or surgeon or judge, and the Count with land to his name enough to cover half a county in England. The discreet sound of music, emanating from the garden, was a backcloth to the very picture of wellbeing, to the uniformly suntanned clients (except for the night-owl authors), carefree, amused and taking culinary excellence in their stride. And tragically unaware that they were the rearguard of a society that the war was to extinguish forever.

Such a restaurant was Gundel and the eponymous pancake is its surviving speciality.

GUNDEL PANCAKES

Serves 6

Pancake batter
1 egg
2 oz (50 g) flour
1/4 pint (150 ml) milk
1/2 oz (15 g) butter, melted
1 oz (25 g) sugar
1 teaspoon olive oil
Dash of vanilla essence
Filling
3/4 oz (20 g) candied orange peel
1 1/2 oz (40 g) raisins
6 fl oz (175 ml) dark rum
4 fl oz (100 ml) double cream

4 1/2 oz (125 g) sugar
7 oz (200 g) coarsely ground walnuts
Pinch of ground cinnamon
Chocolate sauce
4 oz (100 g) dark cooking chocolate
1/2 teaspoon vanilla essence
6 1/2 oz (190 g) sugar
11 fl oz (325 ml) milk
3 egg yolks, beaten
6 fl oz (175 g) double cream
6 oz (175 g) flour
2 oz (50 g) cocoa powder

Filling: Cut the candied orange peel into julienne (long, very thing) slices with a sharp kitchen knife. Soak this and the raisins in rum for 24 hours.

Drain the raisins and orange peel, but reserve the rum. Bring the cream to the boil, add sugar, walnuts, cinnamon, drained raisins and orange peel. Cook, stirring, until it thickens into a paste. Cool this mixture a little and add half of the rum you have reserved.

Sauce: Place the chocolate in a bowl and put in a very low oven, or over a pan of hot water, to melt. Add the vanilla essence and 1 1/2 oz (40 g) sugar to 9 fl oz (250 ml) milk and bring to the boil. Whip the cream, but not too stiffly. Set aside.

Mix the flour and cocoa powder with a whisk, add the remaining cold milk, reheat and keep whisking until smooth and frothy. Add the remaining sugar, the beaten egg yolks and the melted chocolate, and whisk in the hot milk/chocolate mixture. Bring to the boil, remove from the heat and cool a little by stirring. Fold in the whipped cream, and the remainder of the rum. (Reduce the quantity of sugar according to the bitterness of the chocolate.)

Make 12 pancakes, spread on them portions of the walnut preparation, roll them up and coat with chocolate sauce immediately before serving.

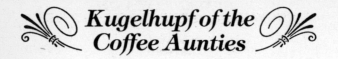

Kugelhupf of the Coffee Aunties

Kugelhupf conjures up the cafés or coffee houses of Vienna and Budapest. I should really call them something else, so different were they from the utilitarian, canteen-evoking image attached to 'café' in English. It would take a whole book to describe and characterise them. The grander ones, with pavement terraces and usually equipped with vast mirrors, were much like the Café de la Paix in Paris, for sitting and browsing, and in the evening for dining. Newspapers from all over the world, on bamboo frames, and leather-bound magazines in umpteen languages, periodically changed from table to table by teenage commis waiters (called piccolos), made them akin to libraries — cheap for the price of a cup of coffee you were allowed to nurse for as long as you liked. Our pubs are typified by their customers and so were those cafés, some known for their regular clientèle of writers and journalists, others for business people, artists, actors or musicians. They were forums for discussing politics, philosophy, music, or for negotiating deals or playing billiards; be it over coffee, a glass of vermouth, frankfurters or a plate of goose liver in aspic.

Some in the sedate part of town were a rendezvous for groups of elderly women who gathered round their regular tables. They would meet day after day at 4 p.m., carefully dressed, gossiping and chattering away like parrots in a cage. Invariably, they drank coffee with a piece of gâteau or pastry which, five times out of ten, was *kugelhupf*, not too rich, deliciously light yet reasonably plain, just the thing with coffee.

Their gossip generally dented reputations; paired off, with raised eyebrows, the less conventional young women; picked others, with a knowing smile, to be blackballed from one party or another. It sounds more sinister than it was: the 'Coffee Aunties', as we used to call them, were merely having what was their idea of fun.

KUGELHUPF OF THE COFFEE AUNTIES

Serves 6

3 large eggs, separated
½lb (225 g) unsalted butter
6 oz (175 g) caster sugar
Vanilla essence

½lb (225 g) self-raising flour
1 heaped tablespoon unsweetened
    cocoa powder
Icing sugar

Preheat the oven to 180°C (350°F) or gas mark 4.

Beat the egg whites until stiff and place on one side.

Mix the butter and sugar and, while beating, add 3 dessertspoons warm water and the vanilla essence. Beat the egg yolks into this mixture, followed by the flour, then fold in the beaten egg whites.

Pour two-thirds of the mixture into a buttered kugelhupf mould, mix the remaining one-third with the cocoa powder and spoon this on top of the mixture already in the mould.

Cook in the pre-heated oven for about 50 minutes to 1 hour until the cake has risen. Turn out on to a plate and dust with icing sugar before serving.

Mint Soufflé with Chocolate Sauce

Judging by the number of semi-emigrés who have settled there, Provence seems to be home from home for the British. If I were 10 years younger I would run my affairs from an ample armchair surrounded by a battery of electronic devices on a shaded terrace in Provence. The food, wines, herbs, restaurants, the climate and much else besides, are a powerful magnet.

So they proved to a French insurance salesman almost 50 years ago when he was still running in the rat race in Paris. Life starts at 40, he decided, and had the strength of character to start a new life in his beloved Provence. But what to do? A restaurant perhaps, as he was a good amateur cook? He started looking and, as he once told me, a tourist official of the region gave him a few good tips, including the stunning location of Les Baux-de-Provence. There our insurance salesman found a decrepit hostelry (*oustaú* in Provençal) ideal to be fashioned to his dreams. The regional tourist official was called Pompidou (yes, the one you think) and the emgiré from Paris was Raymond Thuilier, now the world-famous *patron* of the Oustaú de Baumanière and mayor of Les Baux (he played host to the Queen of England during Pompidou's presidency). About 90 now, he still dons his whites and holds court daily, sitting at the edge of his customary table near the garden entrance, keeping a grandfatherly eye on Jacques Charial, the chef-patron-in-waiting, and exchanging reminiscences with some of his venerable customers.

One of their many unforgettable dishes I have enjoyed under the ancient trees was this soufflé combination.

MINT SOUFFLÉ WITH CHOCOLATE SAUCE

Serves 6

For the soufflé
9 fl oz (250 ml) milk
1 bunch fresh mint, 4½ oz (125 g)
2 oz (50 g) sugar
2 egg yolks
1 oz (25 g) flour
6 egg whites

For the chocolate sauce
4 fl oz (100 ml) milk
2 oz (50 g) double cream
4½ oz (125 g) dark chocolate
1½ oz (40 g) butter
1 small glass of crème de menthe
   liqueur

To make the custard, bring the milk to a boil, add 4 oz (100 g) mint; cover and leave to infuse for at least an hour, then strain the milk through a sieve. Whisk the sugar and egg yolks in a bowl until thick and creamy, then fold in the flour. Bring the mint-flavoured milk to a boil and pour it slowly on to the mixture, stirring constantly until thickened. Pour the custard into a saucepan and heat gently, stirring to prevent it sticking. As soon as the first bubbles appear, remove from the heat and allow to cool. Cover to prevent a skin forming.

Meanwhile chop the remaining mint leaves. When the custard is cold, mix in the chopped mint leaves and 2 soupspoons of the crème de menthe, stirring gently with a whisk.

Re-heat the custard and, at the last minute, whisk the egg whites until firm and fold them quickly but gently (though quite thoroughly) into the custard. Transfer to individual or one large soufflé dish (at least 8″ diameter) that has been brushed with butter and dusted with caster sugar. Fill the dish(es) three-quarters full. Cook in a preheated oven 230°C (450°F) or gas mark 9 for 12 minutes for the individual soufflés; 20–35 minutes for one whole soufflé (which is always better), or until the soufflé has risen.

Chocolate sauce: (this can be made in advance). Heat the milk with the double cream and melt the chocolate in it. Add the butter and 2 soupspoons of crème de menthe. Mix well and transfer to a sauce boat. If the sauce is made in advance, reheat it gently.

To serve, put a little soufflé on each plate and cover with chocolate sauce.

Mocha-and-Walnut Gâteau

No doubt about it: when it comes to pâtisserie, the smell is the thing. You can keep your eye-catching artifices, spun sugar flowers, butter-cream swirls, shaped mountain peaks of whipped cream, punctiliously placed black cherries or pistachio nuts, or the awesome architectural desserts pictured in so many 19th century etchings. All leave me cold. It may be sacrilegious, but the icing on the Christmas cake — and the birthday cake — is totally wasted on me. Forgive me, but I find it cheap. Though it is said that you start eating with your eyes, as far as pâtisseries and chocolate are concerned, I start eating with my nose. Have you experienced small chocolatiers in Paris, making their own exquisite, bitter-chocolate bonbons? The chocolate smell in those shops is as good as the taste.

I also love entering Maison Bertaux in Soho. The tell-tale smell of butter hits me and burns an instant hole in my pocket, in which there is always a blank cheque. There are no frills that could corrupt the unspoilt, puritanical simplicity of the place: all focuses on the goods that Michael, the pastry chef, has been producing for 16 years and Michele has been selling for just as many.

To me, walnut is one of the most sophisticated constituents of desserts, much less obvious than chocolate, less pedestrian than hazelnut, more distinguished and elegantly flavoured than almond and less coarse than its South American cousins. Walnuts are underestimated and underused in the practical, Anglo-Saxon world, perhaps because they are prone to rancidity. In Central Europe, they improve even the most carefully conceived desserts.

Far be it from me to become anthropomorphic about food, but I have to say that another attribute of the walnut's character is its tolerance for racially distant company: it mixes with coffee, its soul brother, comfortably and happily, as in Maison Bertaux's gâteau opposite.

MOCHA-AND-WALNUT GÂTEAU

Serves 6–8

For the sponge
2 medium eggs
2½oz (65g) caster sugar
2½oz (65g) plain flour
For the coffee butter cream
8oz (225g) caster sugar
2½fl oz (70ml) water
1 medium egg, well beaten
8oz (225g) unsalted butter, creamed

2–3 level teaspoons fine coffee powder
To finish
1½ tablespoons rum
5oz (150g) apricot jam, boiled (see below)
10 walnut halves, chopped
Flaked almonds, roasted in the oven until they take on colour

First make the sponge. Whisk the eggs and sugar together until the mixture is light and creamy. Fold in the flour. Pour the mixture into a greased and floured 7" cake tin and bake at 180°C (350°F) or gas mark 4 for 30 minutes, until the sponge is well risen. Turn out on to a wire rack and leave to cool.

To make the coffee butter cream, boil the sugar and water together until a temperature of 115°C (240°F) is reached on a sugar thermometer. Gradually pour on to the well-beaten egg, whisking until the mixture is cool. Add the creamed butter, and then the coffee powder to taste, continuing to whisk until well blended.

Now assemble the cake. Slice the cooled sponge into three equal layers and sprinkle each layer with the rum. Spread the coffee butter cream mixture liberally on to the bottom layer and place a second layer on top. Spread the second layer with the butter cream, reserving some of the cream for the finishing. Add the final layer of sponge and brush the top with half of the hot apricot jam, which has been boiled without water for 1 minute.

Arrange the halved walnuts on the top of the gâteau and brush the nuts with the remaining apricot jam. Spread the sides with the reserved butter cream and mask them with the roasted, flaked almonds.

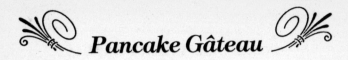

Pancake Gâteau

My passion for pancakes is, I understand, something of a nuisance to my family. I jump at the slightest excuse or opportunity to prepare them or, I should say, suggest that I prepare them, for my offers have been turned down diplomatically but with increasing frequency in recent years. Nowadays, Barbara is rarely moved by my mouth-watering promise of wonders to be created in the frying pan, not to speak of the enticing fillings I conjure up hopefully. It just goes to show that there is such a thing as a surfeit of excellence ...

While passion often gets the better of my culinary balance and I descend to the pedestrian varieties, there are shrewdly thought-out combinations, rich but sumptuously satisfying as well as absorbing fun to do.

My favourite is pancake gâteau, not only to eat but to make, for which the pancakes have to be thicker. Following the detailed routine is absorbing. There is the consistency of the batter, to be adjusted with a drop of milk now and again as the frying proceeds; the careful timing of the cooking only on one side of the pancake, exactly sufficient to keep the reverse side moist and almost — but not quite — uncooked. All this in itself in delicious. Gluttons, however, can make it richer: they add layers of filling which offer opportunities for variations, using the thinnest layers of jam, sultanas, cinnamon, walnuts, even poppyseed!

And then the skill with the oven, so that the gâteau comes out with the top browned yet not crisp; and the skill it takes to plunge a small, very sharp, pointed knife in the centre, in preparation for carving a regular-looking wedge out of a very soft and wobbly mass.

As you can see, when it comes to pancakes, I give up all pretence of being a gourmet and become completely gourmand.

PANCAKE GÂTEAU

Serves 6

3 oz (75 g) unsalted butter for frying
4 oz (100 g) orange marmalade with
   very finely cut peel (or with no
   peel)
3 tablespoons brown Grand
   Marnier liqueur
5 eggs, separated

2 oz (50 g) unsalted butter for
   pancakes
2 oz (50 g) flour
2 oz (50 g) caster sugar
½ pint (300 ml) milk
Grated rind of 1 lemon

Clarify the 3 oz (75 g) butter for frying to prevent it burning when you prepare the pancakes (see recipe for Potatoed Chops, page 112 for clarified butter method). Prepare the orange layer: heat the marmalade and Grand Marnier in a saucepan and set aside to cool a little.

Beat the egg whites until stiff and set aside. Place the egg yolks in a bowl, add 2 oz (50 g) butter and mix energetically until frothy.

Add the flour, sugar and milk to this and mix thoroughly. Then add and gently mix in the stiffly beaten egg whites.

Pre-heat the oven to 190°C (375°F) or gas mark 5.

Heat some butter in a frying pan. Ladle in some pancake mixture of more than normal thickness, about ¼″. Fry this carefully, browning — rather quickly at high heat — one side only and leaving the other side almost uncooked. Slide this onto a tray or large plate, semi-cooked side up. Gently spread onto it the thinnest layer of marmalade mixture and sprinkle a very little lemon rind on top. Follow the same procedure until you have seven layers, but slide the last pancake on top with its browned side uppermost.

Cook in a pre-heated oven for 8–9 minutes and serve immediately.

Pancakes Belle Époque

The French Customs men were adamant. The photographic parapher-nalia needed at the British lunch I had arranged in Paris couldn't pass through. 'But we are giving a lunch Chez Maxim's,' I said. 'Ah! Maxim's!' the officials chanted, and waved us through. Maxim's is still a magic word in France.

Its beginnings were less respectable. It was the place where well-to-do gentlemen took their *petites amies* at the turn of the century and where all the *grandes horizontales* were well known. It was the home of top-hatted figures, the better types in Toulouse Lautrec's paintings, and the marvellous characters in Sem's charming and stylish cartoons. Sem's best is still on the menu cover.

The last proprietor, the late Louis Vaudable, told me that when the place was refurbished after the first world war, a number of gold coins from the last century were found in the recesses of the red-plush banquettes in what is arguably the world's most attractive dining room. Art Nouveau is not my cup of tea, but this dining room, with Whistler's frescoes and acres of mirrors in the curving frames of the period is irresistible.

How fitting that Franz Lehár's librettist should have used Maxim's for one of the scenes in the Merry Widow, immortalising the name in the lyrics. It must be the envy of all restaurant publicists. The late Alex Humbert, the restaurant's greatest chef about whose cooking you can read elsewhere in this book, fittingly named his marvellous and spectacular dessert *Crêpes Veuve Joyeuse* after Maxim's most congenial period. It was a daring thought to cook a soufflé in a pancake so that when the soufflé rises, it opens the pancake which turns automatically into a delicious, natural receptacle.

PANCAKES BELLE ÉPOQUE

Serves 6

For the pancakes
3 oz (75 g) flour
1½ oz (15 g) icing sugar
Pinch of salt
2 eggs
9 fl oz (250 ml) milk, luke warm
1½ oz (40 g) 35 g butter, melted
For the soufflé filling
3 lemons
9 fl oz (250 ml) milk

1 vanilla pod, split in half
  lengthwisc (or 3–4 drops vanilla
  essence)
Small nut of butter
1 oz (25 g) flour
3 egg yolks
8 oz (225 g) icing sugar
Salt
8 egg whites

Pancakes: In a bowl, mix the flour, icing sugar, salt, eggs and milk, mixing gradually with a wooden spoon to avoid lumps. Add the melted butter. Leave the batter to rest for at least 1 hour. Make 12 thin 6″ pancakes. The melted butter in the batter means that it is not necessary to add fat to the frying pan. Keep the pancakes warm.

Soufflé filling: Finely grate the rind of the lemons and macerate it in the juice for 15 minutes. Prepare a *crème pâtissière:* place ¾ of the milk into a saucepan with the split vanilla pod or vanilla essence and butter. Bring to the boil. Draw off the heat then remove the vanilla pod. Thoroughly whisk the remaining milk with the flour, egg yolks, 3 oz (75 g) icing sugar and a pinch of salt, then gradually whisk in the infused milk. Return the mixture to the pan and whisk over a medium heat until it thickens to a mayonnaise consistency. Allow to cool. Whisk the 8 egg whites until firm; fold in the remaining 5 oz (150 g) icing sugar, then fold the egg whites gently into the *crème pâtissière.*

To finish: Fill the pancakes with the soufflé mixture and fold them over gently, barely overlapping — they will open further as the soufflé mixture cooks. Place them onto a lightly buttered heat-proof dish and cook in a pre-heated oven at 220°C (425°F) Mark 7 for 6–8 minutes. Serve immediately.

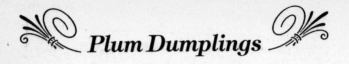

Plum Dumplings

When I was a young boy we used to compare notes as to who could eat the most plum dumplings. It looks barbaric in retrospect, but it was bravado and nothing to young appetites. What enthused us about what appears to be a fairly mundane dish?

You would understand if you had experienced those cold, crisp winters when boys were bursting for activity. We returned, red-faced, with undented energy, from a wild bout of sleighing in the friendly, white mountains around Budapest and crossed the wide Danube in the biting wind on the majestic Elizabeth Bridge; or we walked from the local ice rink. The moment I set foot inside the door, the news reached me: plum dumplings! Never mind the substantial soup gulped down fast to get it over with. There was usually no main course — too much before the treat. And then they made their entrance, heaped on to a large, flat round dish. The characteristic whiff of cinnamon, wafting my way, boosted my appetite powerfully. You started by devouring them with your eyes — there they lay, beautifully round, leaning against each other in their overcoat of browned breadcrumbs. The first helping was three, maybe four. The texture was the thing. I supported the collapsible soft side of the first one with the back of my fork and sank my spoon slowly into the top of the easily yielding pastry, aiming at the middle so as to capture some of the squashy, cinnamon-flavoured plum as well. A blend of textures and flavours burst in my mouth — the soft, comforting, almost purée-like pastry permeated by the sweet taste of the plum it had enwrapped. Then I scooped up some more of the plum, carefully supplementing each spoonful with some of the lard-fried breadcrumbs.

Then the second helping and, perhaps, a third. Downing six or seven dumplings was nothing; nine or ten was quite something; 12 you talked about the next day.

PLUM DUMPLINGS

Serves 6

2 lb (900 g) old, large (not new)
  potatoes that crumble easily
  when cooked
1 egg
1½ oz (40 g) butter for pastry
10 oz (300 g) flour
Salt
1½ oz (40 g) ground cinnamon
1½ oz (40 g) caster sugar

1 lb (450 g) stoned, small plums (they
  must be ripe and sweet)
6–7 oz (175–200 g) fine
  breadcrumbs
1 oz (25 g) butter for frying
  breadcrumbs
Optional:
3–4 oz (75–100 g) ground walnuts

Peel and cook the potatoes thoroughly in salted water. Pass them through a sieve, then cool.

Add the egg, butter, flour, ¼ teaspoon salt and mix well, kneading it into a soft dough. Roll out on a floured pastry board or other, floured, smooth surface to ½″ thickness and cut into 3″ squares.

Mix the ground cinnamon half and half with the sugar and place a pinch of this mixture into each plum. Place a plum into the middle of each pastry square, gather the pastry over them, pinching and sealing it at the top. Sprinkle your hands with flour and roll the pastry packages gently into round dumplings on a floured board.

Shake the breadcrumbs through a sieve and fry in butter to a light brown colour. (As an option, you can mix breadcrumbs half and half with the finely chopped walnuts.)

Place the dumplings, not too many at a time, into boiling water and cook until they surface (approximately 10 minutes). Remove, drain, roll in the fried and browned breadcrumbs (or a breadcrumb and walnut mixture) and serve immediately.

If you cannot get very ripe plums, you can use tablespoons of plum jam instead, but only if it is extremely thick, preferably a variety from Central Europe called 'Povidle'. Or you can use tinned, whole apricots, well drained and stoned.

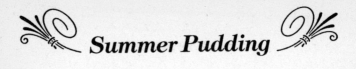

Summer Pudding

'Experts' waste their time arguing whether the Royal Oak in Yattendon, Berkshire, can be rightly called a pub, having regard to its sophisticated restaurant, a few bedrooms and its roaring trade in excellent bar food. What matters is the cooking, which Richard Smith manages to keep mainly English and refined at the same time. A prime example is his famous summer pudding.

I love the feel of the Royal Oak. Its skilled, young waitresses are dashing about, yet the lounge, with its enormous, roaring fire, is very relaxing; its menu is West End-like, yet handwritten; its dining room is polished, yet the furniture transports you into a private house; its cellar is quite admirable, yet you can have just a glass of *any* bottle under £20. That cellar, by the way, owes its excellence to the attractive, efficient Kate Smith (I have always maintained that women have a more sensitive palate than men).

As for the summer pudding, it is one of those dishes for which the recipe has to be arbitrary. The fruit filling depends on the season and, in any case, every home has its infallible custom. Yet, apart from the little technical tricks Richard Smith's recipe describes, it is the choice of fruits and the proportions in which they are used that makes or breaks the dish. It is a spur-of-the-moment shopping decision. That Richard's summer pudding should be widely recognised as exceptional says something for his culinary intuition. What commends itself is the subtle, cunning marriage of the sweeter with the more acidic variety of fruit, a little more of the former and a lighter hand with the latter. Another thing: summer pudding really comes into its own when you eat it al fresco — which you can do at the Royal Oak in the garden.

One thing is essential: lashings of very thick, rich, yellow cream — and to hell with the diet.

SUMMER PUDDING

Serves 5–6
This dish should be started the night before.

4–5 oz (100–150 g) blueberries
4–5 oz (100–150 g) blackcurrants
¹/₂ lb (225 g) raspberries
¹/₂ lb (225 g) strawberries
¹/₂ lb (225 g) redcurrants
¹/₂ lb (225 g) whitecurrants

¹/₂ lb (225 g) caster sugar
¹/₂ large loaf fresh white bread
¹/₂ pint (300 ml) fresh Guernsey
cream
1 sprig of mint

The night before, bury the fruits in caster sugar. Then keep about an eighth of the fruit for garnishing the plates before serving.

Cut the crusts off the bread and discard. Cut the bread into ¹/₂″ thick slices. Line a 7″ pudding basin with the bread slices so they slightly overlap. Fill the basin with the soaked fruit, up to the rim. Put on a lid of more slices of bread and fold over the edges so that it seals the basin.

Press the top down with a saucer; when the juices rise to the top, release the saucer and allow the juices to soak back into the pudding. Place the saucer back on top of the pudding and weigh it down with a weight of 4–5 lb (1.8–2.2 kg). Place in the refrigerator for at least 12 hours.

Turn out the pudding on to a serving dish and decorate with a sprig of mint and some of the fresh fruits. Serve with fresh Guernsey or similar cream, such as clotted or a good double.

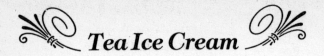

Tea Ice Cream

I n this country an ice cream is an ice cream is an ice cream. Whether it is called vanilla, chocolate or praline, to me it all tastes more or less the same, colour being the only vital difference. Even when the word 'vanilla' is added, and is qualified according to whether it has been made with real cream, the taste doesn't really change.

As a schoolboy I used to watch mesmerised, in my family's restaurants in pre-war Budapest, as the milk, rich with vanilla pods, was boiled, then cooled and chilled, then poured into the huge ice-cream-making machine, furiously and very noisily swirling around in densely packed, well-salted broken ice. After a while, a strong assistant pastry cook immersed a utensil shaped like a gigantic wooden spoon and leaned heavily on its handle, as if it were a rudder. He needed his strength to press the wide bottom end to the internal wall of the spinning vessel, while moving it up and down. This ensured that, as the nectar lining froze, the rest of the liquid got a chance to do the same. That really *was* vanilla ice cream!

I first came across tea ice cream in the house of a film producer whose cook, a young Burmese, produced it as a dessert. As it was announced I thought that the subtle flavour of tea would never in a million years be discernible in an ice cream, but it turned out to be a wonderful preparation. Inevitably, Barbara asked for, and was given, the recipe. We put it down to our ice-cream-making method at home (and eventually to the oriental cook's inscrutability or to our host's jealousy) that our ice cream didn't approach the refined tea flavour at the dinner party. But my hard-headed Barbara, who perseveres in anything difficult she tackles, kept experimenting — adding, subtracting, improving, changing temperatures and freezing times. Two of the main secrets were the choice and the large quantity of the tea. Finally, as always, she came up with the goods.

TEA ICE CREAM

Serves 4–6

6 egg yolks
5¼oz (160g) sugar
2 pints (1.1 l) double cream
6 heaped teaspoons Assam tea

8 heaped teaspoons Orange Pekoe
tea
2 tablespoons dark rum

Beat the egg yolks and sugar together until the mixture has turned a pale colour.

Pour the cream into a saucepan. Place over heat and bring to the boil while stirring constantly. Remove from the heat and add the tea. Stir briefly, cover and leave to infuse for 5–8 minutes. Strain through a fine mesh. Slowly pour the flavoured cream into the egg mixture, beating all the time.

Transfer the mixture to a saucepan. Continue stirring and heat gently, but do not bring to the boil. Cook for a few minutes until the mixture thickens enough to coat the back of a spoon. Remove from the heat and stir for a further 2 minutes, then leave to cool. When cool, mix in the rum and spoon this into an ice cream container.

Set the refrigerator at the coldest temperature. Place the container in the freezing compartment and leave for 2–3 hours. Stir every half hour to prevent ice splinters forming.

Remove 5 minutes before serving.

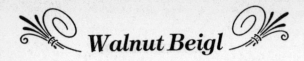

Walnut Beigl

L et me hasten to warn you: this is not to be confused with America's bagel which is not even a poor or modest relative. That's a different story altogether.

We are talking here about the glorious, well nigh ritual Christmas beigl of my country of origin, its importance equivalent to that of Christmas pudding and Christmas cake rolled into one. If I tell you that at the end of the Hungarian Christmas festivities most of us were suffering from what we called beigl poisoning, you will appreciate the symbolic as well as the culinary role it played in our lives.

The main event was dinner on Christmas Eve. 'Ah! The beigl!' — the cry went up around the Christmas table (strictly limited to the family, never ever friends, however close), even at the end of a hefty dinner. Yes, it could be turkey there, too, but not in Catholic households where Christmas Eve was, of course, supposed to be meatless in those days. So it was carp instead, usually fried in breadcrumbs. It was unlike the fat and sickly British carp, lazy and dissipated in peaceful rivers or 'farmed' in lakes.

Beigl was always prepared in quantity, so it would last for many days. No visits over Christmas were devoid of it, and visits were never ending. At tea it was a natural, but even at mid-morning visits (what quaint customs we had!) beigl accompanied the glasses of liqueurs that were de rigueur. You see what I mean about beigl poisoning?

There were two distinct camps: the walnut and the poppyseed faction, apart from the spineless who indulged in both. I could never understand it, being a walnut man myself. However, as a matter of objectivity, here is the brief poppyseed variety of the filling:

Boil 9 fl oz (250 ml) water with 9 oz (250 g) sugar, pour onto 1 lb (450 g) poppyseed. Mix with grated lemon peel, cinnamon, sultanas and two tablespoons of honey. Cool and spread on to pastry.

WALNUT BEIGL

About 20–30 helpings
Wrapped in a kitchen cloth, this will keep for about a week in a cool place.

Pastry

1 oz (25 g) fresh yeast
About 6 fl oz (175 ml) milk (see below)
2 lb (900 g) plain flour
1 lb (450 g) unsalted butter
2½ oz (65 g) caster sugar
Large pinch of salt
2 beaten egg yolks for glazing

Filling

1 lb (450 g) ground walnuts
2½ oz (65 g) sultanas
1 level teaspoon ground cinnamon
Grated rind of a lemon
7 fl oz (200 ml) milk
12 oz (350 g) sugar

Dissolve the yeast in a little warm milk.

Mix the flour, butter and sugar well. Add the yeast, salt and enough milk to achieve a medium textured pastry, neither too hard nor too soft. Leave to rest for ½ hour.

Place the walnuts, sultanas, cinnamon and grated lemon rind in a large bowl. Heat the milk and sugar in a saucepan, stirring constantly, until it comes to the boil. Pour this into the bowl and mix well with the other ingredients. Leave this to cool before spreading on the pastry.

Pre-heat the oven to 180°C (350°F) or gas mark 4. Divide the pastry into six equal portions. Roll each out thinly and spread with the walnut mixture. Roll up, Swiss-roll fashion, trim the ends and place on to non-stick or greased baking trays leaving space between each beigl for some expansion.

Brush the tops and sides liberally with the beaten egg yolks and bake in the oven for about 35 minutes until the top is a deep golden brown. Leave to cool before serving.

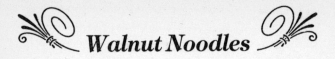

Walnut Noodles

Some of the pasta dishes we used to eat in my youth were very un-Italian — they were served at the end of the meal as a pudding; and they were sweet. It was the quantity that mattered to bottomless teenage stomachs.

I can still smell the sweet aroma of walnut noodles, served after a substantial main course when I came home from school, more than ready for lunch. The morning's lessons were heavy going, from 8 a.m. to 1 p.m., preceded, in my case, by playing the vast organ in our school chapel for half an hour at the daily mass. The school belonged to the Catholic teaching order of the Piarists, much like the Benedictines and widespread in Central Europe. Having unwisely confessed to playing the piano, I found myself to be the school organist for four long years, playing at the daily mass and at two on Sunday. (It put me off church for some time.) The Piarist fathers drove us hard academically, so the hourly, ten-minute intervals between lessons were a volcanic eruption of suppressed energy, but, I am glad to say, not without culinary undertones.

It was the school caretaker's perk to sell bread rolls and milk of which we took advantage sometimes twice in one morning. But what rolls! They came in all shapes: featherlight round ones, called water rolls; the more substantial, crisp Imperial rolls (they were first baked in Vienna); ordinary or giant-sized crescents, the latter equalling four rolls; and there were outsized, very tender pretzels. They were all washed down with cream-topped milk. My favourite was one of a flattened shape with a scrumptious butter flavour. The caretaker exhibited them in a basket of colossal size that he could hardly carry up the stairs. The rolls had never been baked more than one or two hours earlier and we fell on them like pernicious locusts. The last sale was at 11 a.m., yet at 1 p.m. I was starving — and quite ready for a big lunch ending with walnut noodles.

WALNUT NOODLES

Serves 4

This dish should be eaten as a dessert after a light main course.

1 lb 2 oz (500 g) fresh tagliatelle (made with eggs)

6 oz (175 g) ground walnuts

4 oz (100 g) icing sugar

2 teaspoons cooking oil (for the water)

3 teaspoons goose fat or cooking oil

Mix the ground walnuts and icing sugar thoroughly.

Add the cooking oil to 5 pints (about 3 litres) water, bring to the boil and cook the tagliatelle in fiercely boiling water for 4–5 minutes (9–10 for dried pasta). Meanwhile, heat the goose fat (or oil), but do not overheat.

Strain the tagliatelle, give them a quick rinse under the cold tap and strain again thoroughly. Pour the tagliatelle into the fat, keep stirring and heat gently.

Serve the noodles either on meat plates or large soup plates. The walnut-and-sugar mixture should be sprinkled generously on top. Guests should be asked to mix this mixture into the pasta before starting to eat.

After-Dinner Coffee and Chocolate

Sometimes, when there is no risk of appearing to be eccentric, I serve after-dinner hot chocolate, instead of coffee, to our guests. They follow in distinguished footsteps: Richelieu, to mention one of many, loved it, though he made excuses: it was beneficial, he said, against 'vapours of the spleen, biliousness and bad humour'. Brillat-Savarin praised its stimulating effect in times of 'intense concentration', and, of course, it does have a small caffeine content. Millions have a passion for it. The scientific fact is that chocolate is an antidepressant and that it stimulates certain neurotransmitters in the brain; that's why those with a tendency to addiction can get hooked.

The first Chocolate House in London was established in 1657. It sold chocolate for making a cup at home for the then exorbitant price of 15 shillings per pound. London was completely conquered by these thriving institutions in the 18th and 19th centuries. It is inexplicable that the charming and delectable habit should have all but disappeared, eventually giving way to coffee houses.

Coffee came into my life very early. In the intensely aromatic, basement coffee room of my father's immense restaurant complex, the ritual of coffee roasting was enacted every morning at 6.30. As a boy I often watched, transfixed, as the vast amount of roasted coffee was released from the roasting machine into the revolving cooling drums. So coffee holds few secrets for me.

The continental coffee house may be a political talking shop or a Shakespearean Rialto-like market place, mostly a social mix. The Englishman's club is home from home, a refuge and a sharp social divider, where he has a steady marriage with tea to which he looks for solace. Continentals have a passion for coffee and treat it like a lover: they vary it, use it as a stimulant and as a satisfying ending to the meal.

AFTER-DINNER COFFEE AND CHOCOLATE

Coffee

Ingredients (per person)
2 very heaped teaspoons very finely
   ground coffee (a blend of ³⁄₄

light-roasted breakfast coffee
and ¹⁄₄ dark-roasted
after-dinner coffee)

Pour 1 small (after-dinner-sized) cup of *cold* water per person into a saucepan. Add 1 additional cup of water per 6 persons. Add the very finely roasted coffee. Start heating. As soon as it reaches boiling point, remove from the heat. Rest for 30 seconds, bring to the boil again and remove immediately. Rest for 1 minute. Sprinkle very lightly with cold water, then let the sediment settle for 2 minutes. Strain into a pre-heated coffee pot (porcelain, earthenware or copper) and pour into pre-heated cups.

Chocolate

Ingredients (per person)
1¹⁄₂oz (40g) finest dark cooking
   chocolate
1¹⁄₂ heaped teaspoons plain cocoa
   powder (unsweetened)

¹⁄₅ cup milk (for measuring use cup
   in which you will serve it)
¹⁄₅ cup water (same cup)
1 small pinch salt
¹⁄₃ teaspoon sugar

Pour the milk and water into a saucepan and add all the ingredients. Heat and bring to boiling point while whisking. Keep boiling (and whisking) for 30 seconds. Pour into a pre-heated chocolate pot (porcelain or copper) and serve in pre-heated medium-sized cups.

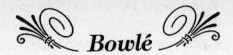

Bowlé

Bowlé has always been a drink for exceptional, exuberant occasions. Perhaps the custom was established at the races at the turn of the century, where it was served at the large, stylish, private parties given by potentates. Style, they say, was the all-important thing in those days, sometimes in an incredibly dramatic form.

There is a horrifying story about one of the legendary Counts Eszterházy around that time. Leading his winner of the Hungarian Derby back to the paddock, he was importuned and pestered all the way by an unknown aspirant insisting on buying the winner, raising the price to absurd heights. Europe's wealthiest landowner, a taciturn and haughty aristocrat unused to being spoken to by strangers, did not dignify the man with a reply. To demonstrate his contempt for financial temptation as well as for strange commoners, he simply pulled out his gun and shot the horse dead.

In my own, somewhat less theatrical times, the exuberant aspect of bowlé occasions still prevailed. I often encountered it not only in some more affluent homes, but also at May Balls. The weather almost invariably permitted them to be held al fresco and we never left much before 6 a.m.

I still serve bowlé at home on occasion, when the chemistry of the gathering is promising. The recipe sounds simple, but has to be executed with great care for detail, especially for the cooling times, and woodruff is a *sine qua non*.

It is only fair to add a word of caution: an incomparably delicious drink in the right circumstances, it is a deceptive potion, misleading to guests who invariably think they are drinking something light. They most certainly are not.

BOWLÉ

Serves 8–10

You will need some tulle material (washed and well rinsed) enough to shape into a small sack to hold the dried woodruff; or you can use one cut-off foot of women's tights (washed and well rinsed, even if new).

1 bottle good quality dry white wine
1 bottle good quality red wine
1 bottle Champagne
4 small to medium-sized oranges
   (preferably blood oranges —
   alternatively ½lb (225g) very
   ripe and very aromatic
   strawberries, (which give the
   best result of all); or 5
   medium-sized, very aromatic
   peaches)

2–4 tablespoons caster sugar
   (quantity according to the
   ripeness of the fruit)
3 tablespoons good brandy
6 tablespoons brown vermouth
5 tablespoons dried woodruff

Chill the white wine, red wine and Champagne the night before.

At least 5 hours before serving: peel the oranges and remove the pith. Cut into thin, round slices, then quarter them and place in a small bowl. (If you use strawberries, wash, remove stems and cut fruit into smallish pieces. If you use peaches, immerse them for 20 seconds in boiling water, pull off the loosened skin, remove kernel and cut fruit into ⅓″ pieces.) Add sugar according to the ripeness of fruit, but do not over-sweeten. Add brandy and vermouth. Leave the bowl in the refrigerator for at least 2 hours.

Pour the contents of the bowl into a large container and add the white wine and red wine. Prepare a small sack (see above), place the woodruff into it and tie the ends tightly with a piece of string, leaving plenty of length by which to pull the sack out of the bowl. Immerse this into the liquid, then pull it out, squeeze out over the liquid and repeat this several times so as to ensure maximum infusion of the woodruff; then leave the sack in the liquid with its extra length of string hanging out. Place this container in the refrigerator. If it is too big, try to cool it by surrounding it with ice in the kitchen sink; or, in the winter, cover and leave out of doors.

Before serving, add the chilled Champagne, and leave it to blend (but keep refrigerated) for 5 minutes. Serve by ladling the bowlé, always catching 2 or 3 bits of fruit, into comfortable wine glasses.

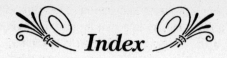

Index

All Sphere Books are available at your bookshop or
newsagent, or can be ordered from the following
address:
    Sphere Books,
    Cash Sales Department,
    P.O. Box 11,
    Falmouth,
    Cornwall TR10 9EN.

Alternatively you may fax your order to the above
address. Fax No. 0326 76423.

Payments can be made as follows: Cheque, postal order
(payable to Macdonald & Co (Publishers) Ltd) or by credit
cards, Visa/Access. Do not send cash or currency. UK
customers: please send a cheque or postal order (no
currency), and allow 80p for postage and packing for the
first book plus 20p for each additional book up to a
maximum charge of £2.00.

B.F.P.O. customers please allow 80p for the first book
plus 20p for each additional book.

Overseas customers including Ireland, please allow
£1.50 for postage and packing for the first book, £1.00
for the second book and 30p for each additional book.

NAME (Block Letters)..

ADDRESS ....

....

☐ I enclose my remittance for_____

☐ I wish to pay by Access/Visa Card

Number ⸻⸻⸻⸻⸻⸻⸻⸻⸻⸻⸻⸻⸻⸻⸻⸻

Card Expiry Date ⸻⸻⸻⸻